BREAKING THE
GRIP

of

Dangerous
EMOTIONS

BREAKING THE
GRIP
_of_
Dangerous
EMOTIONS

JANET MACCARO, PhD, CNC

SILOAM
A STRANG COMPANY

Most Strang Communications/Charisma House/Siloam products are available at special quantity discounts for bulk purchase for sales promotions, premiums, fund-raising and educational needs. For details, write Strang Communications/Charisma House/Siloam, 600 Rinehart Road, Lake Mary, Florida 32746, or telephone (407) 333-0600.

Breaking the Grip of Dangerous Emotions by Janet Maccaro
Published by Siloam
A Strang Company
600 Rinehart Road
Lake Mary, Florida 32746
www.siloam.com

Cover design by Judith McKittrick

Copyright © 2001, 2005 by Janet Maccaro
All rights reserved

Library of Congress Catalog Card Number: 2001087192
International Standard Book Number: 1–59185-787-2

05 06 07 08 09 — 9 8 7 6 5 4 3 2 1
Printed in the United States of America

DEDICATION

To my husband, Michael, and my children Michael, Amanda and Jillian, who came into my life at just the right time. I love you dearly.

ACKNOWLEDGMENTS

I acknowledge that every dangerous emotion that I have experienced in my lifetime has served as a teacher in this schoolroom that we call life. I acknowledge that there is a "divinely orchestrated" time for deliverance. It may be days, weeks, months or years, but deliverance does come. Knowledge will be imparted, and a life is healed. I thank God for the opportunity to write this book from the other side of emotional pain and from a life that is truly healed. I acknowledge that He is my healer and my source from which all things come at "just the right time."

CONTENTS

Contents

Contents

Contents

LIST OF CHARTS AND TABLES

Author's Note

As a child, I remember throwing rocks into the lake near my home. I loved to watch the ripples that encircled the point of entry. These ripples would touch many other objects that floated on the water's surface in close proximity to the initial splash. Because of that big initial splash, many objects, both on the water's surface and below, were changed by the event. I didn't realize then that this simple childhood pastime would one day help me to understand the impact of trauma on my emotional, physical and spiritual health.

This book is a must for anyone who suffers from physical illness, emotional pain or spiritual bankruptcy. It is an account of my own journey through emotional pain and fatigue, which resulted in illness. It is a story of victory over past pain and trauma that will encourage, uplift and arm you with the necessary tools to heal your life and inspire others.

Use this book as a blueprint to help break the grip of past emotional wounds. For the multitudes on drugs for pain, depression, grief and anxiety, this book offers a key to freedom from the chemical straitjacket of prescription drugs. In order for genuine healing to take place naturally, issues must be resolved, the brain must be replenished, the body needs to be rebalanced and the spirit must be reenergized. This book will help you experience life the way God intended it to be.

The mind/body connection is now common knowledge, and researchers from the fields of behavioral medicine, neurology and immunology work together in concert more and more. The field of orthomolecular therapy—which involves treatments that focus on restoring the body's natural chemistry—has exploded. This book provides a useful guide to cutting-edge nutritional supplements and lifestyle changes to set you free from dangerous emotions that destroy your body and mind. The problem is epidemic. This book will turn it around, one reader at a time.

EMOTIONS

We are emotional beings. To experience the full range of emotions—happiness, sadness, hate, love, excitement, boredom, empathy and apathy—is to enjoy the passion of life itself. Without emotions we would be nothing more than robots. We could not enjoy the wonders of this world if we did not have emotions attached to what we hear, say and see. If we never experienced sadness or boredom, how could we relate to or appreciate happiness, joy or excitement? While no one likes to experience dangerous negative emotions, they can serve as catalysts for growth and pathways to a richer existence.

All too often we grow up learning defense mechanisms that hide our true feelings, and we survive by becoming the image of what we believe is acceptable. This image robs us of true happiness. We begin to live lives that others have chosen for us, and we deny the beauty of who we really are.

Emotions are powerful. Take heed because they serve as teachers of what is important in our lives. If you ignore your emotional self, then you will pay a very heavy price. Emotions that are not dealt with can keep you from fulfilling your true divine destiny.

Foreword

I am a big believer in divine guidance. I believe I was led to read this wonderful book by Janet Maccaro, PhD. I am in constant search of answers for people with problems related to anxiety, depression and stress. Still, I never realized the importance of including amino acids such as GABA as part of an overall treatment protocol for anxiety and depression until I read this book. In fact, this book was so enlightening, I found it difficult to put down. *Breaking the Grip of Dangerous Emotions* is an incredible educational self-help tool.

Because of my profession I understand the importance of nutrition in managing anxiety, depression and other emotional challenges. In our program Attacking Anxiety and Depression, we suggest various nutritional supplements. However, I was unaware of the great importance of using many of the natural products that Janet discusses to help *nourish* our brains. Medications for anxiety and depression don't feed or nourish the brain; they simply treat the symptoms and often create unwanted side effects.

If you don't have a clear understanding of brain deficiencies and their relationship to good mental and physical health, you will by the time you finish this book. Science and medical professionals are beginning to understand the importance of looking into the brain to map deficiencies and treat causes instead of merely treating symptoms. There is light at the end of the tunnel for everything from panic disorder to ADHD.

Of course! Doesn't it make sense that a deficiency could cause a problem that could be remedied by correcting the deficiency? If your brain is deficient you need to feed it with nutrients, not medications. In her book Janet cleverly quotes Dr. Billie Jay Sahley as writing, "There is no such thing as a tranquilizer deficiency." I loved that!

I appreciate Janet's easy-to-understand, direct style of communication. She clearly outlines what nutrients are needed for which medical concerns. Whether she is discussing kava, passionflower or St. John's wort, she explains in detail exactly how each works and the best method of dosage. What a complete and informative guide for the layperson or professional seeking an alternative to traditional methods of treatment!

In this wonderful book, Janet guides us through a myriad of physical and emotional problems from emotional fatigue, anxiety and sugar addiction to lupus, premenstrual syndrome and sleep disorders, giving us options that are natural and healthy.

In a world where it often seems difficult to find clear, effective solutions to our physical and emotional pain and suffering, this book is a godsend.

—LUCINDA BASSETT, CEO
MIDWEST CENTER FOR STRESS AND ANXIETY, INC.

Foreword

What are dangerous emotions? They are those emotions that make you feel out of control or that seem to have control over you. Dangerous emotions make you feel less than you are, less than God created you to be. They try to dictate what you do, feel, think and say.

Dangerous emotions include anger, depression, jealousy, fear, boredom, grief and apathy. Surely there are others, but these lead the wolf pack, threatening to devour and destroy us and everyone around us. Emotions were designed to protect us and enable us to experience the world around. Our emotions, together with our logic, register all of our experiences in this world.

We tend to be suspicious of those who are too emotional and those who seem unfeeling because of their lack of emotion. It's when our emotions are too strong, too threatening, too great for us to handle that we feel as if we are falling apart. We are creatures who need balance, and that includes balancing our emotions, our thoughts and our personhood.

At one time or another we all will be in the grip of destructive and dangerous emotions. They may come at the loss of an important relationship or because of our own ill health. They can result from a serious accident or the strain of living with a difficult mate or child. They happen when one lives under great and unrelenting stress for extended periods of time, such as during the terminal illness of a loved one—or even your own. Dangerous emotions occur during financial assaults, a destroyed home or a ruined reputation. Whatever the reason, when dangerous emotions erupt we must respond.

At a time of great difficulty in my own life, when I truly felt as if I had to look up to see the bottom, dangerous emotions were my daily companions. Self-pity, anger, fear, depression, more fear and the strong threat of bitterness would raise their collective ugly head from morning to midnight—and beyond. I felt as if I were slushing through molasses with every step I took. Everything about my life was reeling out of control. I was sleeping more, or not sleeping at all, eating more, exercising less, snapping at friends, talking about dropping out and isolating myself. I was experiencing other kinds of self-destructive behavior, which began to scare me.

Into this dark void came a friend, Dr. Janet Maccaro. She brought not only grace and acceptance of me, but she also brought her expertise. She did not have cookie-cutter solutions, trite words of encouragement or a bumper-sticker theology to give me. Rather, she gave me the benefit of her years of experience and research, and she gave me a shoulder to cry on.

She taught me about the importance of replenishing my brain—feeding it correctly—both in thought and in what I put in my body (including vital supplements). Then we talked about changing my thought patterns. "Taking every thought captive" became my byline. It was hard, and it took commitment and practice—and especially some time—but it worked. My life began to turn around. We found that there were things in my past that needed to be explored and expunged. Together we laughed and played and talked. Janet would prescribe a course of action (for mind, body and soul), and we would talk more. She was a friend, mentor, therapist, nutritionist and encourager.

And now you have the benefit of her expertise and her wisdom and experience. For she too has fought the good fight. She is committed to helping others discover what she has found out—for their good and for the good of those they love. This book will give you a recipe for health, a prescription for living well and encouragement to never give up, and it will answer your questions about, *Now what?*

This book will enable you to break the grip of dangerous emotions and get unstuck to become a free person—and a healthy one in mind, soul and spirit. Read it, follow its advice and then get out there and live life joyfully to the fullest—because you deserve it. It is what God wants for you!

—Dr. Karen C. Johnson
Former Producer and Host, FamilyNet Television

Introduction

It has been said that 50 to 80 percent of all illnesses are psychosomatic in nature. Most of these psychosomatic illnesses are the result of too much daily stress or a stressful traumatic event such as a death in the family, divorce or financial problems. Often people who constantly complain about pains and symptoms are told that their illness is *psychosomatic* or *all in their heads*—nothing is really wrong at all. Psychosomatic actually means that your mind is causing your symptoms or illness. Therefore, it can be very accurate if your past is dotted with unresolved emotional, physical or spiritual pain.

Your mind registers each and every trauma or pain. Just like the proverbial straw that broke the camel's back, if you don't deal with painful issues as they occur, they simply pile up, waiting to resurface at some later point. Hurt and unresolved issues are stored one upon another in your overwhelmed mind until one more "straw" is tossed upon the pile, and BINGO!—a chain of body symptoms begin to occur that baffles the best doctors.

These symptoms only worsen, and your life is dramatically impacted. Panic attacks, depression, generalized anxiety disorder, muscle spasms, insomnia and breathing problems can become your constant companions. What makes these suppressed emotions so

1

dangerous is that down the road the immune system breaks down and very real, very serious illnesses start to occur. The two big ones are heart disease and cancer.

Are you one of the millions of people in this country who are or who have suffered from emotional, physical or spiritual emptiness? First, know that you are not alone. Remember that there are millions who are suffering in silence in this country. I was one of them!

The purpose of this book is to educate you on this very real body/mind connected epidemic that has given birth to the Prozac and Xanax generation. You will learn to trace the causes of your emotional or physical illnesses and discover how to get free. In addition, you will learn how to regenerate your brain and body to once again experience balance. I will give you a protocol for stress-related illness. You will also learn how you can come out of emotional darkness and into the unconditional love of God.

I have taken this journey before you and can tell you that your life will be changed forever. You must be patient, for you did not get this way overnight. Healing happens systematically and very gradually. Past unresolved emotional traumas must be identified and released. You must forgive those who have harmed you in the past and learn to be thankful that God has made you a survivor. Learn to put the victim role behind you. You are not a victim. Rather you are someone who has survived in spite of deep emotional wounding and unrelenting stress.

This book will give you hope, rebuild your health and put you on the road to happiness by addressing your body, mind and spiritual health.

PART ONE
REPLENISH THE BRAIN

CHAPTER 1

Start Right Where You Are

Staggering numbers of Americans presently suffer daily from a full spectrum of destructive symptoms. In this chapter we will look at the effect that dangerous emotions such as stress, trauma and anxiety have on the function of your brain.

- 4 million Americans endure a constant state of fretfulness called generalized anxiety disorder (GAD).
- 3.5 million war veterans, crime victims and others with traumatic histories struggle with the terror of *posttraumatic stress disorder.*
- 11.5 million of us are *phobic,* spending large amounts of our lives avoiding situations that make us quake.
- 1.5 million fight heart-pounding, stomach-churning anxiety episodes known as *panic attacks.*
- 2.5 million suffer from *obsessive compulsive disorder* (OCD) in which nightmarish thoughts can only be suppressed by repetitive rituals such as hand washing and housecleaning.

MY STORY

THE FIRST PANIC ATTACK

It was a happy occasion, a celebration. My husband's new office was finished. I had spent several months totally remodeling an old cottage while at the same time trying to meet a difficult business deadline. During that time I was also studying for my master's degree in nutrition, raising three children, recovering from a hysterectomy, dealing with relationship problems and—last but not least—coping with the unexpected return of my father. He had come back to my hometown after leaving my mother, brother and myself some thirty years before.

I was maxed out from taking care of everyone else's needs, which left little time to care for my own.

I lived with little sleep, high stress, even higher adrenaline levels and with little or no exercise. Emotionally I was a wreck, but I didn't even have enough time to realize it.

So, as I prepared for the celebration I called my attorney and invited him to stop by to see the new office. He invited my husband and me to meet him at a nearby restaurant, which we gladly did. As I entered the restaurant, I felt a little strange, out of sorts—a bit uneasy. I dismissed it, figuring that my blood sugar was probably low or I was simply tired and worn out from the day.

It was then I noticed that every muscle in my body was tense—so tense, in fact, that I struggled hard to breathe. *Odd,* I thought as we sat down at the table. As the waitress brought the menus I pretended that I was just fine, but all the while a sense of impending doom and disorientation closed in around me. I started to experience a choking sensation—my throat felt as if it was swelling and closing shut. My hands and feet began to tingle, I was extremely short of breath, the room started to spin, and I felt as if I would faint or even die!

I tried to calmly excuse myself and headed for the front door. I was weak and gasping for breath as I walked out to the parking lot. Suddenly I was chilled to the bone as my blood pressure plummeted.

When my husband came out to check on me, I told him that I

6

thought I was having a stroke, a heart attack or that I was dying. Whatever was happening, there was no way I could go back into that restaurant. I did not want to go to the hospital either, so I just had my husband drive me home.

At home I lay still, totally wiped out for what seemed to be hours. My pulse was weak and faint; my blood pressure remained low. I felt a little better the next morning, thank God, but I remained weak for a while.

After a week passed, I finally asked, *What was that? What caused that? Will it ever happen again?* Well, the answer to the third question was YES, it did happen many more times before I understood what caused it.

What I had experienced is commonly known as a *panic attack.* This experience began a painful, agonizing journey into emotional pain that started in childhood and followed me into adulthood. As you read my story, I want you to think about your own situation. Do you suffer from anxiety, depression or a chronic or devastating autoimmune disease such as fibromyalgia or lupus?

If so, go back in your mind to find where your emotional trauma began, perhaps as far back as your childhood. Ninety-nine percent of my clients who deal with chronic disease and anxiety disorders in adulthood have been through a great deal of stress, emotional trauma and psychological pain. Circumstances may feel just fine in your life at the moment. Even so, do you often feel anxious, depressed or hopeless? Do you try to hide your emotional or physical unwellness, only to see it intensify?

There is only one way to heal—let it out and let it go. Acknowledge your pain and give it to God. To get free, regeneration must take place in your body, mind and spirit. Your healing will not happen overnight. Mine did not. Getting well body, mind and soul will be a daily process. By walking through this wilderness experience you will accomplish three things:

· A closer walk with God
· A better understanding of yourself
· A better appreciation for life in general

You will learn to stop and smell the roses. Better still, the fragrance of those roses will seem even more intense and their color more beautiful when you get to the other side of pain and illness. You will have walked through the pain to get to a new life in which you find joy in meeting each new day.

You will learn to be an overcomer.

THE ROAD BACK

Let's begin.

For a period of about five years my panic attacks came and went. Only now do I understand what caused them. I was dealing with too many life changes. In five years time all of the following events happened to me:

- I had two major operations.
- A family member lost everything he owned to drugs.
- My father, who came back into my life after thirty years, died shortly after from brain cancer (I took care of him).
- My son left home for college.
- My middle daughter rebelled.
- My younger daughter experienced learning problems.
- My husband needed a new office, of which I oversaw the remodeling.
- We had marital problems due to all of these other situations.
- I was pursuing a master's degree and then a PhD in nutrition.

Add in my type A personality for good measure, and that's all, folks! These panic attacks did land me in the hospital three times and at the cardiologist's and family physician's offices much more often. The doctors told me that stress was the cause and offered a pill or capsule to calm my mind and body.

This explanation was unacceptable to me. It was during this time that my faith in God grew deeper as I drew closer and closer to Him. In prayer, I asked for the strength to endure these attacks, the wisdom to know what to do about them and the courage to continue on. God did give me all of the above. Clearly, this was something He wanted me to walk through, for no instant healing came.

What did come, however, were clients. I was a nutritional consultant at this time, and no one knew what I was going through. I thank God that it was not externally evident. I began noticing a bizarre pattern in many of the individuals with whom I worked. Initially they came in for nutritional consultations. All of them were suffering with some autoimmune, chronic or stress-related disorder. I began to feel as if I were seeing the same person over and over again. Their health profiles were remarkably similar.

I repeatedly saw the same symptoms charted by these clients—insomnia, depression, anxiety, poor digestion, muscle aches and pains, headaches, neck and shoulder pain in addition to chronic diseases such as lupus, fibromyalgia, Crohn's disease and irritable bowel syndrome.

Another thing these individuals had in common was that they were all great givers of themselves. They all had full lives with many responsibilities. As I began designing programs for these people, I covered all the bases concerning nutrition. However, I began to feel compelled to ask if they felt the need to share any additional information that might help me to make their programs more effective. That's when an "ocean of emotion" began to erupt. I heard tales of rape, divorce, sexual abuse, abandonment, isolation and even murder!

These individuals who were suffering so severely in their physical bodies had emotional pain and trauma in their pasts that they thought they had overcome or had simply chosen to bury deep inside. As each heart-wrenching story emerged, my heart went out to them. I understood their pain because I too had experienced emotional trauma in my own life.

As I researched this emotional connection to physical illness and stress disorders, information found its way to me that was truly life changing. I will share this information with you together with my prayers that you will see the light at the end of the tunnel. Emotional illness and resultant physical illness can be devastating. For some, this can be especially true.

I have had several pastors' wives call me with feelings of guilt as they shared their stories of illness, depression and anxiety. These women feel especially lonely and isolated because they can't give themselves permission to be sick or unhappy—for after all, they are the "pastor's wife." How would it look to the congregation if the pastor's own wife had problems? These women tended to pretend to be just fine. They wore a smile and suppressed their own emotional pain. They felt all used up, and they felt as if they had failed their husbands. Most of all, they felt that they had failed God. Most of them secretly thought that their illnesses were some sort of punishment.

Such thinking only makes illness worse. You can climb out of your emotional abyss and live a victorious life! I did it, and so have many others. Recovery starts with knowledge. To be truly set free you must get armed with understanding that will help you to recover.

> My people are destroyed for a lack of knowledge.
>
> —HOSEA 4:6, KJV

THE ROLE OF STRESS

No matter what condition you are in, whether you are suffering from stress, fibromyalgia, panic attacks, muscle tension, lupus, chronic fatigue syndrome or depression, just remember one thing: Your current state of health developed over many years. The good news is that even though you may feel defeated, you still have a level of good health. God has kept you and will continue to do so. I believe that God allows us to grow and mature spiritually through adversity.

Where do we begin? I do not intend to inundate you with a lot of technical information. Instead, I will try to educate you and gently direct you back on course. You will be surprised to see how much better you will feel just by understanding why you feel the way you do. This journey I have taken before you. With the knowledge and restoration comes the responsibility to share and teach you from my heart.

To whom much is given, from him much will be required.
—LUKE 12:48, NKJV

I will now lay out a blueprint for rebuilding your body and brain after years of stored trauma and stress. First, let's find out just how much emotional stress and pain are contributing to your current state of health. Take this test developed by the Midwest Center for Stress and Anxiety. There are common backgrounds in people who suffer from anxiety and chronic illness.

YOUR STRESS LEVEL

Check the boxes that apply to you:

CHILDHOOD:

- ❏ Unstable upbringing
- ❏ Lack of approval and praise
- ❏ Feeling that you must prove yourself
- ❏ Strict religious upbringing/guilt and fear
- ❏ Siblings parenting other siblings
- ❏ Nervous disorders in family
- ❏ Separation, divorce of parent or loss of a family member
- ❏ Strict parents with high expectations
- ❏ Family history of alcoholism
- ❏ Low self-esteem
- ❏ Feelings not easily shown or displayed

COMMON TRAITS

There are several personality traits that are adopted because of our childhood experiences. The following traits are commonly found in people who suffer from anxiety and stress-related disorders.

Check the ones with which you can identify:

- ❏ Tendency to overreact
- ❏ Perfectionist
- ❏ Inner nervousness
- ❏ Emotionally sensitive
- ❏ Guilt ridden
- ❏ Extremely analytical
- ❏ Overly concerned about others' opinions of you
- ❏ Obsessive thinker
- ❏ Worry about health problems
- ❏ High expectations
- ❏ Inability to make decisions

THE BODY/MIND CONNECTION

When your emotional pain turns into full-fledged anxiety, you may experience any of the following symptoms.

- Fatigue
- Muscle tension
- Strange aches and pains
- Migraine headaches
- Depression
- Dizziness
- Hot and cold flashes
- Nausea
- Racing heart
- Disorientation
- Panic attacks
- Scary thoughts
- Sweats

FOUR LEVELS OF STRESS

Now let's look at the four levels of stress. This will help you to determine what level of stress you are experiencing:

LEVEL 1

- Losing interest in enjoyable activities
- Sagging of the corners of the eyes
- Creasing of the forehead
- Becoming short-tempered
- Bored, nervous

LEVEL 2—ALL OF LEVEL 1, PLUS:

- Tiredness
- Anger
- Insomnia
- Paranoia
- Sadness

LEVEL 3—ALL OF LEVELS 1 AND 2, PLUS:

- Chronic head and neck aches
- High blood pressure
- Upset stomach
- Looking older

LEVEL 4—ALL OF LEVELS 1, 2 AND 3 PLUS:

- Skin disorders
- Kidney malfunction
- Frequent infections
- Asthma
- Heart disease
- Mental or emotional breakdown[1]

Come unto me, all ye that labor and are heavy laden, and I
will give you rest.

—MATTHEW 11:28, KJV

EMOTIONAL FATIGUE

Emotionally fatigued people are everywhere—you may be one of
them. Emotional fatigue is another manifestation of stress.

I was emotionally fatigued for many years as I searched for
answers to my many physical complaints. These included Epstein-
Barr virus, systemic yeast infections, hormonal imbalance,
endometriosis, low blood sugar, chronic fatigue syndrome and
more. One traumatic experience after another over the course
of several years brought me to the place of complete emotional
fatigue coupled with an underactive immune system.

Those traumas began early in my life. When I was twelve, I
lived with prolonged uncertainty and illness after my parent's
divorce. I covered up the hurt by throwing myself into academics
and sports. I tried to make everyone think that I was just fine. As
a matter of fact, I aimed for perfection in everything I did. This
caused me so much internal stress that physical symptoms erupted
during my teens.

Still, I always felt as if I had to succeed at impossible goals that I
imposed upon myself. I did this to feel accepted. For many years I
was able to keep it going, never letting on that there was an empty
place in my heart where a father's love was supposed to be.

I know now that daughters need their father's love to validate
them. The most precious gift a father can give his children is to
love their mother completely so that the children feel safe, secure
and loved. This gives children a loving example to follow when
they marry. It also gives them a good foundation from which to
build their own families.

Husbands, love your wives, even as Christ also loved the
church.

—EPHESIANS 5:25, KJV

13

I began to realize the toll that extreme emotional fatigue and pain were having on my life during the days in which I cared for my father. He had just been diagnosed with inoperable brain cancer shortly after he returned to town. He passed away after nine short weeks.

I was asked to fly to New York to give his eulogy during a memorial service. I was physically and emotionally drained, but I hopped a plane with his eulogy tightly clutched in my hand. A few years earlier I had rededicated my life to Christ and to serving Him in a mighty way. I believe that this accounted for the fact that even though I was physically, emotionally and mentally exhausted, spiritually I felt stronger and surer of my faith than ever before.

I realized that to heal the many years of abandonment and emotional pain, the eulogy I gave had to forgive my father and let him go. As I stood before the mourners who attended the service, I realized how aware they all were of the circumstances of my childhood. Surely they were wondering if my words would be bitter.

Instead, I gave a tribute to my father that was filled with love, which I will share with you here. It was the beginning of my journey back to emotional wholeness. It was a release that broke the chains of emotional pain that hindered me from living a full, vital life. I am in awe at the transformation. To forgive is divine!

Here is the eulogy I read at my father's funeral:

> Losing a father is one of the most heartbreaking things that can happen to a daughter or son. In my case, this is the second time I experienced the loss of my father.
>
> As a child, it was hard for me to comprehend how my earthly father could choose, through divorce, to no longer be a part of my life. Many milestones in my life have been shadowed by the lack of my father's presence. I am, however, here tonight to honor my father.
>
> I chose long ago not to be a victim, but instead to be an example to the multitudes of others that struggle with the rejection and pain that come from divorce. You can find

inner peace. Tonight, I stand before you to thank my earthly father because the lack of his presence proved to be a catalyst for me to draw closer to my heavenly Father, who will never leave or forsake us.

My walk with the Lord is the most important thing in my life. You see, this was a gift my father unknowingly gave to me, and I am eternally grateful. I believe that the Holy Spirit held me up in the last few weeks of my father's life. I feel truly blessed that the Lord allowed me, for the first time in years, to actually help my father by physically taking care of him, touching him, holding him, lifting him and praying by his bedside just before he took his final breath. Yes, I loved my father, and I do believe that in his heart he did have a place for me and my brother.

Many of you have wonderful memories of my father, and by listening to your memories I am only now getting to know more about him.

I thank God for allowing me to be there at the end for him. I'll always remember that he was there at the beginning for me.

Dad–I have no bitterness or regrets, nothing but appreciation for all of the trials and triumphs, sorrows, pain and disappointments, as well as joys and happiness that were my lot to experience.

One is never forgotten as long as there are those who remember him with fondness. One is never gone if one showed kindness, affection, unselfishness, patience, loyalty, friendliness, helpfulness, sympathy and generosity. Any of these acts have earned you a piece of immortality and eternal gratitude from those whose lives have been touched by yours.

Death is not an end but a beginning of a new and more glorious life with the Lord. May my earthly father rest safely in the arms of our eternal Father in heaven.

While I delivered my father's eulogy to the large group of my relatives and my father's friends, I felt as if angels stood on either side of me as I spoke. Afterward a few teary-eyed people approached and said that they hoped their son or daughter would be as forgiving of them when their time came. In that crowd of mourners were a few people who left their children through divorce also. One of them came to me and said the children always suffer the most. I agreed. I then added that by forgiving their parents, children could be set free from years of stored emotional pain.

Recently I came across an interesting landmark study about children of divorce. This study tracked children from broken homes for a quarter of a century and found that the negative impact of divorce continues well into adulthood. According to Judith Wallerstein, founder of the Center for the Family in Transition in Corte Madera, California, divorce marks children for life. She believes that divorce abruptly ends a youngster's childhood, filling it with loneliness and worry about their parents. Divorce recklessly thrusts tender children into adulthood!

Interestingly, Wallerstein contends that it is in adulthood that children of divorce suffer the most. Even in good relationships, grown children of divorce expect disaster and overreact to mundane differences and trivial conflicts. Wallerstein also predicts a backlash by the children of divorce against deadbeat fathers who now are approaching their senior years. She feels bitter children may threaten to withhold both financial and emotional aid that is often needed in old age as a sort of revenge or payback for the father who was not there after divorce. This is a pretty grim prediction based upon the 50 percent divorce rate these days. It's a scenario that could possibly leave a huge senior generation estranged from their children.[2]

> For if ye forgive men their trespasses, your heavenly Father will also forgive you: but if ye forgive not men their trespasses, neither will your Father forgive your trespasses.
>
> —MATHEW 6:14–15, KJV

When I took care of my father during his final days there were moments that I felt angry, cheated, hurt and abandoned. But as each of his final days passed, I chose forgiveness, not bitterness. Because of my decision to love instead of hate, I was set free and saved from past pain; I now look forward to a life of emotional wellness. How you react is your choice. Choose love, forgiveness, mercy and compassion, for it will come back to you one hundred times over!

In the days and weeks that followed the memorial service, I felt an incredible release. I really thought I was on the other side of the emotional pain when suddenly, I began to experience extreme lethargy and then panic attacks, headaches, shortness of breath, dizziness, insomnia, backaches and bronchitis. Every muscle in my body felt tight as a piano wire. I was so drained and achy that I noticed myself always leaning against a wall just to hold myself upright. I found myself crying often—something I never let myself do as a child.

Suddenly I had no control over my emotions. They were clearly controlling me! Unpleasant as it was, it was the beginning of my journey back to emotional wellness. I began to find wonderful books and resources—or should I say they found me. Lucinda Bassett, through her tape series Attacking Anxiety, helped me to understand the reasons I was suffering and how to control my panic attacks.[3]

As you read on in this book you will find protocols for rebuilding and regenerating your body, mind and spirit. One important thing to remember is that you must be patient and let peace come slowly. You will have wonderfully peaceful days and some anxious ones. It is going to take some time to rebuild your body and your nerves. Time is a great healer. So, let go of the struggle, stop suppressing your emotions and begin expressing yourself.

Pray daily, share everything with God, confess your sins and repent of them. You'll be forgiven. Next, forgive others; let go of all resentment, bitterness, jealousy or envy. I can't emphasize this enough. These emotions only tear your body down. It has been said that each one of these emotions can make you more susceptible to degenerative disease, especially to cancer, heart disease and arthritis.

THE WORLD'S OLDEST QUESTION—WHY ME?

If you are someone who is dealing with emotional or physical unwellness as a result of dangerous emotions, you have probably asked, *Why me?* After all, you are human, and it is certainly a valid question. In this first section, I will begin to unravel this question like a big ball of yarn—one inch at a time. I will begin by educating you about the effect that emotional pain has on your brain.

In my own case, I suffered from post trauma, otherwise known as posttraumatic stress disorder. As I mentioned, after my father's return to town and his death shortly afterward, I endured anxiety attacks that ranged from mild to severe, along with the entire list of anxiety-related symptoms. It was not until I began to delve deeper into my emotional health that I realized I had suppressed my emotional hurt and the pain of my parents' dysfunction and resultant divorce. I had been plagued with physical illness that began in childhood and followed me into adulthood, including hormonal imbalance, shingles, Epstein-Barr virus, systemic yeast infections, strep infections, endometriosis with resultant hysterectomy, mitral valve prolapse, heart murmur and low blood sugar.

Nevertheless, my physical problems were a walk in the park compared to the emotional pain and anxiety I endured. I often felt lightheaded and weak. My legs felt weak and unsteady when I walked. I often had difficulty breathing. My heart would race, pound and skip beats. My lips and fingers tingled. I got chronic headaches, neck aches, shoulder pain and low back pain. Often I felt tired, weak and lacking in energy. I couldn't relax easily. My muscles twitched and went into spasms, and I even experienced a choking sensation.

At times I truly felt as if my life was not worth living. It was only my faith in God that kept me afloat and encouraged in what I now consider my days in the valley.

I read and researched anything I could find on physical and emotional depletion. Before long I encountered information that I found fascinating about the depletion that occurs not only in the body but also in the brain as a result of anxiety, panic, grief, stress and strain over the course of many years. I read about the work of Billie Jay Sahley, PhD, and the research of Candice Pert, PhD, in the field of orthomolecular nutrition, which included supplementation with amino acids to restore the brain following the emotional and physical depletion. Over time, anxiety, suppressed emotional pain, unresolved anger, grief and unforgiveness can deplete the brain of amino acids, which are crucial for optimal brain chemistry.

With this knowledge, I had finally stumbled across the starting point on my journey back to emotional, physical and spiritual health.

THE BRAIN

While panic and anxiety attacks involve the brain, they are also felt throughout the entire body, for our brains control every cell in the body. The brain is responsible for all our thought patterns, movement, behaviors, unresolved anxiety, emotional pain and traumatic memories. When a person experiences crippling panic attacks or emotional illness, there seems to be biological and possibly genetic factors involved. These contribute to the many different physical symptoms that accompany stress and anxiety reactions. It seems that our perception of traumatic events or stress can actually alter our brain's chemistry.

Neurotransmitters, which are important chemical messengers of the brain, help to control our feelings of anger, fear, anxiety and depression. But when these very important neurotransmitters are depleted, prolonged anxiety or trauma can overload the cerebral cortex of the brain, causing release of adrenaline that floods the brain and triggers a multitude of life-disrupting physical symptoms.

This can lead to eventual immune system breakdown. Because fear, anxiety and other dangerous emotions can alter the brain and body's chemical balance, they have a profound influence on the development of illness.

THE LIMBIC SYSTEM

The limbic system is located deep within the brain. In the limbic system you will find the thalamus, amygdala, hypothalamus and the cortex. It is this system that deals primarily with behavior and emotions—this is the emotional storehouse of the brain where anxiety is born. The amygdala is involved in some of the most complex functions in the brain, namely emotions and memory.

Pychosomatic disorders are mind/body connected. By this I mean that they are transmitted from the brain to the skeletal system, which can translate them to the nervous system and the muscles. This extremely tensed state interferes with proper sleep and eventually leads to fatigue and emotional despair or breakdown.

In other words, the brain becomes depleted just as our bodies do. So, it follows that by supplementing our brain with specific nutrients—which are needed for the brain to create new neurotransmitters—we can replenish, recharge and regenerate the brain while simultaneously focusing on nutrition to rebuild the body. This discovery literally changed my life.

In the past, I was able to keep my body in balance through diet and specific supplements that were targeted to my particular areas of concern. However, this discovery about brain replenishment proved to be the missing piece of the puzzle. With this piece in place, my healing became total and complete.

Your healing can begin right now, right where you are. As you continue reading you will discover how to add the missing pieces your body needs to operate in optimal health.

CHAPTER 2

Add the Missing Pieces

Amino acids are the building blocks of protein. Just how important are they? Your body depends on the twenty-nine different types of amino acids to form sixteen hundred basic proteins that compose 75 percent of the body's solid weight of structural, muscle and blood protein cells. Amino acids are responsible for the growth, repair and maintenance of our bodies. Most importantly, they are sources of energy that play a vital role in brain function.

You can imagine my excitement when I read that an amino acid deficiency in the brain could be responsible for today's epidemic of anxiety, pain, stress and emotional fatigue. Your brain and body cannot function without amino acids. These powerful substances just may be the new medicines that will replace the Xanax, Prozac and Valium of the twenty-first century.

Amino acids heal and restore brain function because they control the anxiety stop switch, function as a muscle relaxant and act as pain relievers. More importantly, amino acids create new neurotransmitters for proper brain communication, helping you to think better, feel better and stay healthy.

In her book *The Anxiety Epidemic*, Billie Jay Sahley, PhD, stated, "There is no such thing as a tranquilizer deficiency." Some six to ten million people in the United States alone suffer daily from anxiety attacks, fear, panic and phobias, according to Sahley. Annually, these folks swallow about 982,550 pounds of medication and spend a whopping $875 billion on Xanax, Zoloft, Prozac and Valium.

MIND MEDICINE

Here is a list of the most commonly prescribed antianxiety medications and their side effects.

BENZODIAZEPINES

* Xanax
* Valium
* Ativan
* Klonopin

These medications are normally prescribed for a few weeks straight. They work by boosting GABA, which damps the overactivity of the central nervous system. The downside is that they are strongly habit forming, and they are hazardous if taken with alcohol or other sedatives. In addition, they may cause birth defects if taken early in pregnancy.

SSRIs (SELECTIVE SEROTONIN REUPTAKE INHIBITORS)

* Paxil
* Zoloft
* Prozac
* Luvox

These are usually prescribed for social anxiety disorder and general anxiety disorder (GAD). They enhance the effect of the neurotransmitter serotonin. Known as antidepressants, their side effects include nausea, dizziness, headaches and decreased sexual function.

MAOs (MONOAMINE OXIDASE INHIBITORS)

* Nardil
* Parnate

These antidepressants require cautious use. They can interact with common foods and drugs to cause dangerously high blood pressure.

VENLAFAXINE

· Effexor

This boosts the effects of serotonin and norepinephrine. Common side effects are drowsiness, nausea and sexual dysfunction.

TRICYCLICS

· Elavil   · Tofranil
· Anafranil

These are older antidepressants that are generally used when the newer drugs are not effective. They are more likely to cause side effects than newer drugs. These side effects can range from drowsiness to potentially lethal irregular heartbeat.

BUSPIRONE

· Buspar

This boosts serotonin levels, thereby quelling anxiety. The downside is that it can take up to eight weeks to kick in completely, so it is not recommended for panic disorders.

Medication can dramatically improve any anxiety symptoms you may have, and as you can see, there are many drugs from which to choose. As with any medication, side effects can also impact your quality of life.

While these medications can be of help for a short period of time, total mental, physical and spiritual health must come from replenishing, restoring and rebuilding the brain, body, mind and spirit.

THANK GOD FOR GABA

Of all the neurotransmitters in the brain, GABA, or gamma-aminobutyric acid, is the most widely distributed. It has a very important part to play in the regulation of anxiety.

During my own experience, I used GABA to replenish my brain, thereby calming my mind and body. Its effect was truly amazing.

When my GABA receptors were replenished, the false alarms or "overfirings" stopped, and the panic attacks ceased.

I have since recommended GABA to my clients who continued to have mind and body symptoms long after they completed their nutritional programs. The results were no less remarkable. GABA proved to be invaluable in the quest for emotional balance and freedom from anxiety and stress-related illness. This was because the GABA receptors in the area of the brain that control anxiety became replenished and restored after supplementation with this simple amino acid.

Traumatic memories can be stored throughout your body. Your brain is not the only organ that suffers. Your stomach, skin, muscles, heart, skeletal system and any other organ of your body suffer as well. Since there are GABA receptors throughout your entire body, it is believed that taking GABA in the proper amounts can reduce the stress, anxiety and tension throughout your body.

Many of my clients who complain of stomach trouble almost always have a stress or trauma connection that is unresolved. According to Dr. Sahley's research, your gut has a brain, which is located in the lining of the stomach, esophagus, small intestine and the colon. The brain in your head communicates with the brain in your gut.[1] Here comes the mind/body connection once more.

Dr. Michael Gershon, a professor of anatomy and cell biology, reported in a *New York Times* article dated January 23, 1996, that many gastrointestinal disorders like colitis, irritable bowel syndrome and diverticulitis can originate from problems within the gut's brain.[2] In essence, diarrhea, nausea or constipation can be a result of prolonged anxiety, stress or emotional pain. This is because the brain in your head communicates with the brain in your gut by way of the neurotransmitters.

GABA is normally abundant throughout this complex network of the mind and body. When the GABA supply is deficient, the brain suffers and your body is flooded with uncomfortable life-disrupting symptoms. So it is very possible that your present behavior, state of mind or physical health is a direct result of your stress levels, anxiety, grief, anger, unresolved conflict and resultant deficiency of GABA.

The following chart will show you just how much anxiety and trauma—both past and present—can deplete your GABA supply.

TRAUMA DEPLETES GABA

If GABA receptors become low or empty, symptoms occur throughout the body. Emotions that deplete GABA include:

- Pain
- Grief
- Anger
- Fear
- Anxiety
- Panic

These unresolved emotions lead to chronic pain, illness and other physical symptoms. In addition, the following anxiety-related symptoms also appear:

- Panic attacks
- Difficulty breathing
- Rapid heartbeat
- Headaches
- Crying
- Back pain
- Insomnia
- Neck pain

How GABA DEPLETION AFFECTS THE ENTIRE BODY

- *Eyes*—pupils dilate, blurred vision
- *Mouth*—dry mouth, choking sensation
- *Heart*—racing, palpitations, pounding
- *Lungs*—difficulty breathing, bronchioles constrict
- *Stomach*—contracts, nausea, indigestion
- *Adrenal glands*—release adrenaline, weak, no energy
- *Colon*—gas, constipation, diarrhea
- *Bladder*—frequent urination

GABA is the main inhibitory neurotransmitter that restores the brain. Its function is to regulate anxiety, muscle spasms, depression and chronic stress. But there are other nutrients that work along with GABA for its proper metabolism.

MAGNESIUM

One nutrient in particular is magnesium. Magnesium enhances GABA's action and effect on the body. Interestingly enough, most people with long-standing anxiety and stress problems are deficient in magnesium. Furthermore, it is important to note that the symptoms of magnesium deficiency are the same as those that occur with anxiety, stress and emotional depletion.

I have listed the symptoms of magnesium deficiency. Compare them to the chart that lists stress and anxiety symptoms, and you will see a very real connection begin to emerge.

MAGNESIUM DEFICIENCY

· Depression	· Muscle spasms
· Anxiety	· Panic attacks
· Mitral valve prolapse	· Fibromyalgia
· Fatigue	· Low blood sugar
· Irregular heartbeat	· Dizziness
· Headaches	· Constipation
· Irritable bowel syndrome	· Asthma
· Spastic symptoms	· Chronic pain
· Noise sensitivity	

Do you see the similarity? According to many different experts, while GABA replenishment is something that can replace some of the most over-prescribed medications of our day such as Prozac, Xanax, Valium and other similar mood-altering drugs, magnesium enhances the effect even more.

This is life-changing information. Throughout the years that I suffered physical illness and anxiety symptoms I always believed that the answer would find its way to me. Thanks to these pioneers in amino acid and GABA research, Dr. Candace Pert and Dr. Billie Jay Sahley, it did!

WHEN STRESS SHATTERS, MAGNESIUM SAVES

When you are chronically stressed, you can become magnesium deficient, even if you eat foods that are rich in magnesium daily. When you are exposed to continuous stress you become irritable, easily fatigued and lose your ability to concentrate. In addition, your blood pressure may increase because your level of adrenaline increases in your blood. Under these conditions of mental or physical stress, magnesium is released from your blood cells and goes into your blood plasma. From there it is excreted in the urine.

A study conducted in France found that this stress-induced depletion of magnesium was more dramatic in those with type A personalities, who were competitive and prone to heart disease.[3]

Some believe that this depletion of magnesium among type A individuals is the primary reason why they are at increased risk of heart attacks. Interestingly, when an individual suffers a heart attack, magnesium is administered immediately.

Because I am your typical type A personality with a family history of heart disease, I have made magnesium a very important part of my daily dietary supplement protocol. Magnesium taken by mouth is very safe, except if you suffer from kidney disease or if you are severely dehydrated. In these situations you could develop levels of magnesium in the blood that are simply too high. If you are in doubt, check with your healthcare provider. Taking too much magnesium also may cause drowsiness and lethargy.

I wholeheartedly recommend supplementation. We Americans consume diets that fail to meet even the government's minimum recommended dietary allowance for magnesium. Most troubling is the lower-than-average magnesium intake among individuals who develop heart disease.

I personally take and recommend 400 milligrams of magnesium at bedtime. I prefer a gel capsule to a hard tablet. Because magnesium is the most critical of all minerals for coping with stress, in addition to taking a supplement, add the following magnesium-rich foods to your diet:

MAGNESIUM-RICH FOODS

• Almonds	• Bananas
• Blackberries	• Black-eyed peas
• Broccoli	• Dates
• Green beans	• Kasha (buckwheat)
• Kidney beans	• Millet
• Navy beans	• Shrimp
• Soybeans	• Tuna
• Watermelon	

When stress and dangerous, health-robbing emotions threaten to destroy the delicate balance of your body, shield it with magnesium. To summarize, heart attacks, high blood pressure and other stress-related diseases that run rampant through our society today have one common thread—magnesium deficiency. Make magnesium a part of your recovery protocol and continue to take it as insurance to protect you during stressful times. This is especially true for type A individuals.[4]

HORMONAL HELP FROM PROGESTERONE

Progesterone and GABA—a match made in heaven. If you've read any of my other books, you know that I am fan of natural progesterone. Here is yet another reason why this wonderful gift from God is a blessing to your well-being. Progesterone is important to your central nervous system. It is concentrated in brain cells in levels twenty times higher than that of blood serum levels. According to John R. Lee, MD, in his book *What Your Doctor May Not Tell You About Menopause,* such high concentrations in brain cells cannot be due to simple diffusion but require work on the part of the brain cells.[5] This alone strongly suggests that progesterone in brain cells must serve some important purpose.

Progesterone has a calming or mildly sedating effect on the brain. Lee feels that this effect may be caused directly by progesterone, or substances created from progesterone that are active at GABA receptors may cause it.

Remember, you learned earlier that GABA is a neurotransmitter inhibitor that has a calming effect. See the connection? In my own case progesterone not only evened out my severe hormonal imbalance, but it also helped to calm my anxious mind while promoting a sense of well-being. When I added GABA to my health-building protocol, the difference was truly amazing.

If you are a women going through premenopause or menopause, natural progesterone can balance out the roller-coaster ride of hot flashes, irritability, mood swings, headaches, fatigue, foggy thinking and more. In addition, it will help alleviate anxiety and the nervous

28

symptoms associated with this season of life. For more information, see the product source section at the back of this book under Dr. Janet's Balanced By Nature Progesterone Cream.

THE 100-BILLION-DOLLAR QUESTION

Right now you may be asking yourself, *Why isn't everyone that suffers with anxiety, depression and the related disorders told about GABA? If it is so wonderful, why doesn't everyone jump on the GABA bandwagon?* I'll just say this: GABA is a naturally occurring amino acid. Natural substances cannot be patented and therefore do not create enormous profits. Enough said?

> Do not remember the former things, nor consider the things of old. Behold, I will do a new thing, now it shall spring forth; shall you not know it? I will even make a road in the wilderness.
>
> —ISAIAH 43:18–19, NKJV

NATURAL TRANQUILIZER AMINO ACIDS

In addition to GABA and magnesium, the following amino acids also help to restore and replenish the brain. Some amino acids act as major inhibitory neurotransmitters. These include the following:

LYSINE

Lysine is an essential amino acid effective in the natural treatment of hypothyroidism, Alzheimer's disease and Parkinson's disease.

GLUTAMINE

This amino acid is a prime brain nutrient and energy source. Supplementing your brain with glutamine can rapidly improve memory, recall, concentration and alertness. It helps to reduce sugar and alcohol cravings and controls hypoglycemic reactions.

TYROSINE

This is a wonderful semi-essential amino acid formed from phenylalanine. Tyrosine helps to build the body's natural supply of adrenaline and thyroid hormones. It is also an antioxidant and is a source of quick energy, especially for the brain. Because it converts in the body to the amino acid L-dopa, it is considered a safe natural support for Parkinson's disease, depression and hypertension. Avoid tyrosine if you have cancerous melanoma or manic depression.

GLYCINE

Glycine helps to release growth hormone when taken in large doses. It converts to creatine in the body to retard nerve and muscle degeneration. It is wonderful for controlling and regulating hypoglycemic symptoms, especially when taken in the morning upon rising.

TAURINE

A potent anti-seizure amino acid, taurine is a neurotransmitter that helps control the nervous system and hyperactivity. It also works to normalize irregular heartbeats, helps prevent circulatory and heart disorders and helps to lower cholesterol. Since the natural sources of taurine are hard to find, supplementation is the best way to receive adequate amounts for therapeutic benefit.

GUIDELINES FOR TAKING AMINO ACIDS

· Take amino acids with their nutrient cofactors for the best uptake.
· Take amino acids before meals with the exception of brain stimulant amino acids.
· Make sure to take amino acids with plenty of water for optimum absorption.

Please note that active forms of amino acids are the only ones available for sale. Even if you do not see an "L-" (levo) or "D-" (dextro) before the amino acid, the product is still in its active form (example: L-carnitine or carnitine).

Once you have discovered that amino acids play a vital role in your brain's health, you will be ready to understand the important link between your brain and your emotions.

CHAPTER 3

The Chemical Equation Linking Brain and Emotions

Your emotions are not just "all in your head"! Your emotions are linked to the chemistry of the immune system. Stress-coping skills are needed to help immunize our bodies against emotional assault.

THE MIND/BODY CONNECTION
HOW EMOTIONS COMMUNE WITH YOUR IMMUNE SYSTEM.

Lymph nodes: Small, bean-shaped organs that act as storage compartments for white blood cells.

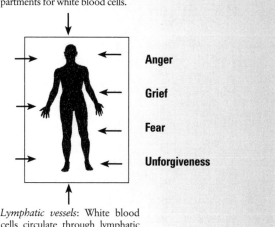

Thymus: T-cells migrate from bone marrow to the thymus to fight off invading organisms.

Bone marrow: Soft tissue in bone cavities where white blood cells are produced.

Spleen: A storage tank for white blood cells.

Anger

Grief

Fear

Unforgiveness

Lymphatic vessels: White blood cells circulate through lymphatic vessels that link the lymph nodes and other immune organs.

31

EMOTIONAL STRESS
LEADS TO IMMUNE SUPPRESSION

Candace Pert, PhD, professor at the Center for Molecular and Behavioral Neuroscience at Rutgers University, made this statement in her research on the entire physiology of the body: "The chemical processes that mediate emotion occur not only within our brains, but also at many sites throughout the body, in fact, on the very surfaces of every single cell."[1]

Early in Dr. Pert's career she discovered a way to measure chemical receptors on cell surfaces in the brain. At this particular time Dr. Pert was studying opiate receptors in the brain, which act like keyholes for opiate drugs such as morphine.

It is the binding of an opiate to its receptor that creates the emotion of euphoria. Soon after, it was discovered that the body makes its own opiates called *endorphins,* which serve as natural painkillers. Our body releases these endorphins or painkillers during events such as childbirth and traumatic injury. Later on, it was discovered that a host of other receptors besides opiates were found in the brain, along with other natural chemicals called *neuropeptides* that fit them.

However, not all neuropeptides are associated with emotions as strong as euphoria. Some are more subtle according to Dr. Pert. This groundbreaking information shocked the scientific community. The fact that endorphins were found in the immune system and that opiates and other receptors were found distributed in parts of the body outside the brain gave the mind/body connection credibility. This new research challenged the old notion that the immune system was independent of the nervous system.

Opiate receptors found in the brain were also found on immune cells. This opened the door and gave birth to mind/body medicine. It is common knowledge today among researchers that the brain and immune system communicate with one another. Studies suggest that even short bouts of dangerous emotions may alter some aspects of immune function.

When dangerous emotions are not dealt with, or emotionally troubling situations become chronic or inescapable, the immune system suffers and health problems arise. People under stress are more susceptible to illness due to the mind/body connection. By taking an active role in the recovery of your mind, body and spiritual health, you have taken a crucial step in changing your life.[2]

THE DISORDERS

When dangerous emotions are allowed to fester within us and we neglect to replenish our brain and body, full-blown emotional disorders erupt. The following disorders have become commonplace. Each one of them is caused by brain, body and spiritual depletion. Experts agree that life events, stress, grief, anger and heredity affect the body's internal chemistry and contribute to the development of the following disorders.[3]

GENERALIZED ANXIETY DISORDER (GAD)

Anxiety and worry seem to be a normal part of our everyday lives. Excessive anxiety causes more than just butterflies in your stomach. It disrupts your life, interferes with your performance and triggers physical discomfort.

GAD is marked by excessive or unrealistic worry about health, money or career prospects that lasts for six months or longer. Keep in mind that realistic anxiety, such as financial concerns after losing a job, is to be expected. However, if you worry excessively over events that are unlikely to occur, you may be struggling with GAD. People who live with GAD typically have a number of physical and emotional complaints including insomnia, dizziness, concentration problems, sore muscles, restlessness and irritability. Symptoms can vary from person to person, but at least six of these indicators must be present for a diagnosis of GAD.

More than five out of every one hundred people will develop GAD at some point in their lives. Researchers have not identified a cause for GAD, but biological factors, life experiences and family background connections appear to play a part. The disorder tends to occur in the early twenties but can also begin in childhood. Others report having their first battle with GAD after age thirty.

Again, too much stress often triggers this disorder. In the months or years immediately prior to the onset of GAD, many sufferers report an increase in stressful life events such as illness, job loss, death in the family or divorce. Positive life events can also be stressful. Happy occasions such as marriage, a new baby or a new career can also be a catalyst in the development of GAD.

While medications can be extremely helpful in the treatment of GAD, my MANTLE technique, commonly known as *progressive muscle relaxation,* has been very successful in helping GAD sufferers. (See page 75 for more information on my MANTLE technique.) Other helpful strategies include exercising for thirty minutes daily, massage, prayer and controlled breathing. Of course, GABA, magnesium and the full spectrum of amino acids will help to replenish the brain and body. Relief does not happen overnight. It will take some time and dedication to achieve lasting results.

SOCIAL ANXIETY DISORDER

This is more than just a case of being shy. Shy people may be extremely self-conscious, but they do not experience crippling feelings known as anticipatory anxiety, avoidance behavior and physical symptoms.

Social phobia is an anxiety disorder that tends to begin in the mid-teen to late-teen years and can grow worse over time. The central fear in this disorder is embarrassment over the way one might act while performing a task in public. An example would be public speaking, which is the most common. Others include the fear of parties or celebrations, eating in restaurants, flying in a full plane or riding in a bus or car.

Social phobics are acutely aware of physical signs of nervousness such as trembling, blushing and sweating. Sufferers feel so much extreme anxiety over upcoming public encounters that their nervousness can create poor performance. This only intensifies future worry. Researchers believe that this disorder is caused by biological or genetic factors along with environmental elements, such as experiencing a publicly embarrassing or humiliating experience at an impressionable age.

Thirteen out of every one hundred Americans have a chance of developing this disorder at some point in their lives. Phobias can disrupt family life, limit productivity, reduce self-esteem and break the spirit. The standard treatments for this disorder include medications, behavior therapy, relaxation techniques and cognitive therapy. Training in social skills is of additional benefit.

OBSESSIVE COMPULSIVE DISORDER (OCD)

Lather, rinse, repeat—persons with OCD feel they must perform some ritual or routine to help relieve their anxiety about their obsessions. Some sufferers spend hours bathing, shampooing, washing their hands or cleaning their homes. These ritualistic behaviors interfere with the person's daily activities.

People with OCD have a fear of uncertainty, have constant doubts and seek reassurance from others. Evidence suggests biological factors may play a part in the development of OCD, and there is a tendency for it to run in families. Many people with OCD also suffer from depression. This can be a very tiring disorder.

Experts believe that OCD is a neurobiological illness that is influenced by life events. It does respond to treatment, and help is available. People who hide this condition from others are suffering needlessly.

RECOGNIZING OBSESSIVE COMPULSIVE DISORDER SYMPTOMS

If you suspect that OCD may be affecting the quality of your life, take the following quiz.

YES NO

❑ ❑ Do you have unwanted ideas, images or impulses that seem silly, nasty or horrible?

❑ ❑ Do you worry excessively about dirt, germs or chemicals?

❑ ❑ Are you constantly worried that something bad will happen because you forgot something important, such as locking the door or turning off appliances?

❏ ❏   Are you afraid that you will act or speak aggressively when you really don't want to?

❏ ❏   Are you always afraid that you will lose something of importance?

❏ ❏   Are there things that you must do excessively or thoughts you must think repeatedly in order to feel comfortable?

❏ ❏   Do you wash yourself or things around you excessively?

❏ ❏   Do you have to check things over and over again, or repeat them many times, to be sure they are done properly?

❏ ❏   Do you avoid situations or people you worry about hurting by aggressive words or deeds?

❏ ❏   Do you keep many useless things because you feel that you can't throw them away?

❏ ❏   Have you experienced changes in your sleeping habits?

❏ ❏   Do you feel sad or depressed more days than not?

❏ ❏   Do you feel disinterested in life?

❏ ❏   Do you feel worthless or guilty?

Reprinted by permission of the Anxiety Disorders Association of America.

You may see your physician or therapist for medication tailored to your needs. Again, the depletion must be addressed. GABA, B vitamins and Brain Link can be of tremendous help. When the brain is restored, emotional issues can be resolved.

POSTTRAUMATIC STRESS DISORDER (PTSD)

With PTSD, your past literally comes back to haunt you. One in ten women suffer from this disorder, which in the past was thought to affect only combat veterans. Now this disorder is affecting women, probably because "women are more sensitive to potential danger, more vulnerable to normal anxiety and more vulnerable to anxiety disorders in general," according to Laura Miller, MD, chief of women's services at the University of Illinois in Chicago.

Every one of us, both male and female, looks backward at times. Thinking about happy moments from our past makes us feel good. But other memories have the opposite effect when there are things in our past that we didn't handle so well and wish that we could have a second chance.

When a death or some other personal tragedy happens in our

lives, we may mourn and ask why. Eventually, we put the past aside and get on with our lives. But some people have a harder time than others moving forward. These people are affected so profoundly by these experiences that they cannot live a normal life.

PTSD is characterized by irritability, being constantly vigilant and having nightmares or flashbacks of a traumatic event in your life. If PTSD becomes a chronic problem, brain depletion occurs because stress can change even the structure of the brain. In addition, high blood pressure, cancer and heart disease have been associated with this condition if left untreated.

DO YOU HAVE PTSD?

Have you experienced or witnessed a life-threatening event that caused intense fear, helplessness or horror? Do you reexperience the event in at least one of the following ways?

Yes No

❑ ❑ Repeated, distressing memories and/or dreams

❑ ❑ Acting or feeling as if the event were happening again (flashbacks or a sense of reliving it)

❑ ❑ Do you have intense physical or emotional distress when you are exposed to things that remind you of the event?

Do you avoid reminders of the event and feel numb, compared to the way you felt before, in three or more of the following ways?

❑ ❑ Avoiding thoughts, feelings, or conversations about it

❑ ❑ Avoiding activities, places or people who remind you of it

❑ ❑ Blanking out important parts of it

❑ ❑ Losing interest in significant activities in your life

❑ ❑ Feeling detached from other people

❑ ❑ Feeling your range of emotions are restricted

❑ ❑ Sensing that your future has shrunk (for example, you don't expect to have a career, marriage, children, normal life span)

Are you troubled by two or more of the following?

❑ ❑ Problems sleeping

❑ ❑ Irritability or outbursts of anger

❑ ❑ Problems concentrating

❑ ❑ Feeling "on guard"

❏ ❏   An exaggerated startled response

❏ ❏   Do your symptoms interfere with your daily life?

❏ ❏   Have your symptoms lasted at least one month?

Self-test reprinted by permission of the Anxiety Disorder Association of America.

The events most likely to trigger this disorder are the unexpected death of a close friend or relative, being assaulted or raped. These are experiences that happen to a large number of Americans. Other triggers include auto accidents, a cancer diagnosis, miscarriage and traumatic childbirth.

The most common symptoms of PTSD are flashbacks, fear and insomnia. There are other troubling symptoms as well. These include symptoms such as jumping out of your skin when someone enters a room and avoiding people, places, smells and clothes that remind you of a traumatic event. In some cases you may even avoid intimacy because you simply can't get close to anyone sexually—or even in general.

When you are suffering with PTSD, you keep a wall up between yourself and the world. If your symptoms of PTSD linger for more than a month, chances are they are likely to become chronic and will begin to cause a ripple effect into all areas at your life.

If you see yourself in several of the PTSD profile chart symptoms, take immediate action to avoid chronic PTSD. Remember, chronic disorders of any kind create brain and body depletion that eventually drains your spirit.

So, what do you do? Where do you start? Begin by talking. The best thing you can do after any traumatic event is talk about it. At the same time feed your brain amino acids. Again, GABA, Brain Link and magnesium will help to create new neurotransmitters. Follow my yeast-, sugar- and dairy-free eating plan. Focus on your adrenal health and follow the protocol. If you feel that you need additional help, you may call the Anxiety Disorders Association of America (ADAA) at (240) 485-1001 or reach them at www. adaa.org. The address is 8730 Georgia Ave., Suite 600, Silver Spring, MD 20910.

Health Magazine stated that one leading cause of posttraumatic stress disorders is a serious car crash. This is because medical caregivers must focus only on the physical trauma while neglecting the emotional issues associated with serious injury. When it comes to PTSD, the sooner issues are addressed, the less emotional suffering has to be endured, which includes vividly reliving the crash, an exaggerated fear of cars and emotional numbness.[4]

One in seven people has experienced a panic attack in the past year. By one estimate, forty-six million people will meet the American Psychiatric Associations criteria for anxiety disorder at some point in their lives. THIS IS AN EPIDEMIC!

PANIC DISORDER

Nearly 1.6 percent of adult Americans, or three million people, will suffer from a panic disorder at some point in their lives. These numbers are scary enough to make anyone panic!

Have your emotions or your stress load gotten so out of hand that panic attacks have become a part of your life? If you suspect that you may be suffering from panic disorder, answer the following questions:

ARE YOU TROUBLED BY PANIC DISORDER?

YES NO

❑ ❑ Have you experieced repeated, unexpected attacks during which you are suddenly overcome by intense fear or discomfort for no apparent reason?

During this attack, did you experience any of these symptoms?

❑ ❑ Pounding heart

❑ ❑ Choking

❑ ❑ Sweating

❑ ❑ Chest pain

❑ ❑ Trembling or shaking

❑ ❑ Nausea

❑ ❑ Dizziness

❑ ❑ Shortness of breath

❑ ❑ "Jelly legs"

❏ ❏   Feelings of unreality or being detached from yourself'

❏ ❏   Fear of losing control or going crazy

❏ ❏   Fear of dying

❏ ❏   Numbness or tingling sensations

❏ ❏   Chills or hot flashes

❏ ❏   Fear of places or situations where getting help or escape may be difficult, i.e. in a crowd or on a bridge

❏ ❏   Being unable to travel without a companion

For at least one month following an attack, have you:

❏ ❏   Felt persistent concern about having another one?

❏ ❏   Worried about having a heart attack or going crazy?

❏ ❏   Changed your behavior to accommodate the attack?

Panic disorder is highly treatable once it is diagnosed. This disorder appears to run in families and is two to three times more likely to strike women. As with other anxiety disorders, the first attack often is preceded by a stressful event such as the death of a parent, a move to a new city or the breakup of a marriage.

It is vitally important to understand what type of anxiety disorder you may have so that you and your healthcare professional can determine the most effective treatment for you. If you decide to try brain-replenishing amino acids like GABA, keep in mind that with panic disorder you may need medication initially to stop the attacks. Over the long term, GABA and the full spectrum of amino acids, along with dietary changes, emotional release and spiritual growth, will ensure positive results.

When dangerous emotions get the best of you, there are four traditional forms of treatment. Most people respond best to a combination of the following four options.

1. *Behavior therapy* helps a person cope with difficult situations, often through controlled exposure to them— for example, holding a spider when you have a fear of spiders or flying when you are terrified of flying. This therapy helps a person modify and gain control over unwanted behaviors. An individual is permitted to be

actively involved in recovery, and the skills learned are useful for a lifetime. Results can take time, however.

2. *Medication* helps to resolve symptoms and restore chemical balance. Medication is effective for many people and can greatly support other treatments. Most of these medications have side effects, however.

3. *Relaxation therapy* includes breathing retraining, exercise and other skills. It can help you to cope daily with the stress that contributes to anxiety. It can take time to achieve results, but it nets powerful results when you become an active participant in your healing.

4. *Cognitive therapy* helps you to change unproductive thought patterns. It helps you to examine your feelings and learn to separate realistic and unrealistic thoughts. It may take a little time to achieve results, but the skills you will learn through cognitive therapy will be useful for a lifetime.

THE MEDICATION MAZE

Most anxiety disorders have a biological component and often respond to medication. These medications can be used over the short term, or they may be required for a lengthy period of time. With the reduction of anxiety symptoms, it is easier for an individual, alone or with a therapist, to find the root cause of his or her emotional distress. By addressing the brain depletion and core issues, the chance for recurrence is greatly reduced.

When you do not deal with anger, resentment, grief, frustration and unforgiveness as soon as they occur, you set yourself up for a future filled with emotional suffering and brain and body depletion and illness. Before your emotions turn on you and devastate your life and the lives of those you love, stop, let go, forgive, sleep enough, eat right, exercise and take care of your "temple." If you don't, you too will be one of the millions of Americans who need medication just to function day to day.

41

GLOSSARY OF MEDICINES

Once dangerous emotions have depleted your brain and body, the following medications are routinely prescribed to help with symptoms.

1. *Anticonvulsants,* often used to prevent or stop seizures, are also used to treat social phobia.

2. *Benzodiazepines* are effective against generalized anxiety disorder (GAD). Some drugs in this category are also used to treat panic disorder and social phobia. They are relatively fast acting. The most common side effect is drowsiness, but they have a potential for dependency. Persons taking benzodiazepines can experience a return of their anxiety symptoms when the drug is discontinued. They may also experience temporary withdrawal symptoms. These problems can be minimized by teamwork on the part of the doctor and patient.

3. *Beta blockers* are often prescribed for those with social phobia. These drugs reduce anxiety symptoms such as heart palpitations, sweating and tremors along with controlling anxiety in public situations. Beta blockers reduce blood pressure and slow the heartbeat.

4. *Monoamine oxidase (MAO) inhibitors* are used in the treatment of panic disorder, social phobia, PTSD and OCD. They require dietary restrictions, and some doctors prefer trying other treatments first. Individuals taking a MAO inhibitor must avoid other medications, beer, wine and certain foods, including cheeses that contain tyramine.

5. *Selective serotonin reuptake inhibitors (SSRIs)* are considered a first line of treatment for panic disorder, social phobia, OCD, PTSD and GAD. They are the newest medicines available for treating any of the anxiety disorders. Traditionally, they have been used to treat depression.

Because you only need to take SSRIs once a day, they have become among the most widely used drugs in the world. Common side effects are mild nausea and sexual dysfunction, which may resolve over time.

6. *Tricyclics (TCAs)*, first created for treating depression, are also effective in blocking panic attacks. They reduce symptoms of PTSD and can be effective against OCD. Tricyclics take about two to three weeks to take effect. The most bothersome side effect is weight gain. Drowsiness, dizziness, dry mouth and impaired sexual function are the other most commonly reported side effects.

Medications can be very helpful in the treatment of stress, anxiety and depression. Nevertheless, while they may be effective, they carry side effects, risks and can be addictive. These drugs only treat the symptoms. If you discontinue these drugs, the symptoms return and you are back to square one. That is very depressing!

NATURAL ALTERNATIVES

Many health professionals are proponents of the use of GABA for anxiety-prone individuals. GABA actually fills the GABA receptor sites in the brain while drugs merely attach to the receptors. Proponents also know that by restoring the brain chemistry with GABA and other amino acids, the brain becomes balanced. This is more desirable than just suppressing the symptoms with the current anxiety drug *du jour.*

GABA came to the rescue in my life and continues to keep my brain chemistry finely tuned. My personal definition for GABA:

G—God
A—Always
B—Brings
A—Answers

Life is meant to be fully lived with all of your senses sharp, clear and intact. Zoloft, Prozac, Paxil and Effexor suppress all feelings of pain, fear, happiness and depression. This is because they block excitatory messages as well as use available serotonin, which affects your mood and perception of pain. When your emotions are suppressed by medication, it's difficult to function at work and home.

In a sense, medication causes you to live life from a dull, suppressed perspective. With amino acids such as GABA, the root problem can be corrected. Your mind and senses will not be dulled, and you will not have to worry about becoming addicted. Extensive research by psychopharmacologists in the last twenty years supports the theory that when the brain is given adequate amounts of amino acids, which are the building blocks for neurotransmitters, behavior is normal. If you are deficient, you may have a constant anxiety problem. All the more reason to be sure that your body is getting plenty of amino acids.

It is possible to live life fully without the dulled perspective of an overly medicated mind. You can learn to overcome the effect of stress on your brain—naturally. In the next chapter we will discover nature's bountiful supply of natural, wholesome supplements to improve your brain health.

CHAPTER 4

Overcoming the Effect of Stress on Your Brain

L earn to recognize early signs of stress and anxiety before life-disrupting symptoms take hold of your mind, body and spirit. Take the following life event test. If you score high or moderately high, it is wise to begin immediately to replenish the GABA receptors in your brain with supplemental GABA. Also remove caffeine, sugar and fatty or fried foods from your diet. Follow the recommended eating plan I have designed for you. You must fortify your body and brain so that you are able to handle your stress and not be destroyed by it.

The stress scale quiz reveals that stress is indeed cumulative. Recognize this fact and diffuse your stress before this ticking time bomb explodes and you are faced with a serious health problem or stress-related disorder.

A score below 150 points means that statistically you have a 30 percent chance of developing a significant health problem in the near future. A score between 150 and 300 points gives you a 50 percent chance. A score of more than 300 points raises the possibility of significant health problems to a whopping 80 percent. By implementing methods for coping with stress, you do not have to be a statistic—you can be an overcomer instead.

LIFE STRESS RATING SCALE[1]

Event	Point Value	Score
1. Death of spouse	100	_____
2. Divorce	78	_____
3. Marital separation	65	_____
4. Detention in jail	63	_____
5. Death of close family member other than spouse	63	_____
6. Major personal injury or illness	53	_____
7. Dismissal from job	47	_____
8. Marriage	50	_____
9. Marital reconciliation	45	_____
10. Retirement	45	_____
11. Major changes in health or behavior in family member	44	_____
12. Pregnancy	40	_____
13. Sexual difficulties	39	_____
14. Major business readjustment	39	_____
15. Major change in financial status	38	_____
16. Death of a close friend	37	_____
17. Change in occupation	36	_____
18. Change in number of arguments with spouse	35	_____
19. Going into debt for major purchase	31	_____
20. Foreclosure of mortgage or loan	30	_____
21. Major change in responsibility at work	29	_____
22. Son or daughter leaving home for college or marriage	29	_____
23. Trouble with in-laws	29	_____
24. Outstanding personal achievement	28	_____
25. Spouse begins or ceases work outside the home	26	_____

26. Beginning or ceasing formal schooling. . . . . 26 _____
27. Major change in living conditions,
for example, new home, remodeling, etc. . . . . 25 _____
28. Revision of personal habits . . . . 24 _____
29. Trouble with your boss . . . . 23 _____
30. Major change in working hours or conditions . . . . . 20 _____
31. Change in residence . . . . 20 _____
32. Change in schools. . . . . 20 _____
33. Major change in usual type or amount
of recreation . . . . 19 _____
34. Major change in church activities. . . . . 18 _____
35. Taking a loan out for smaller purchases . . . . 17 _____
36. Major change in social activities. . . . . 18 _____
37. Major change in sleeping habits. . . . . 16 _____
38. Major change in family get togethers . . . . 15 _____
39. Major change in eating habits. . . . . 15 _____

THE FIGHT-OR-FLIGHT RESPONSE

Exactly what happens to you when you experience stress? The rate of your breathing increases to supply necessary oxygen to the heart. Your heart rate increases to force more blood to the muscles and brain. Your liver dumps more stored glucose into your bloodstream to energize your body to increase your level of physical activity. You produce more sweat to eliminate toxic compounds produced by the body and to lower your body temperature.

Learning to respond with relaxation is crucial to reduce stress. Here is a relaxation response in summary. The heart rate and blood pressure are reduced. The rate of breathing decreases because oxygen demand is reduced when a person is relaxed. The stomach produces more hydrochloric acid, which aids in digestion. The liver secretes less glucose, and blood sugar levels are reduced.

So you can see that it's far more desirable to live in a relaxed state where your body is not working overtime. To achieve this you must exercise, use good nutrition, implement the lifestyle changes outlined in this book, practice the MANTLE technique, commonly called *progressive relaxation*, and consciously focus on God—not on your problems.

Recognize the early signs of stress, and take action early through exercise, relaxation, dietary changes and prayer. Don't let stress become a destructive force that robs you of your quality of life and well-being.

DANGEROUS EMOTIONS DRAIN YOUR BATTERIES

When your emotions have gotten the best of you, it's not uncommon to feel drained or as if your batteries are dead. In a sense, it's true. When it comes to restoring your system after grief, prolonged pain syndromes, anxiety, depression, anger and hostility, your adrenal glands play a vital role.

Your adrenal glands are the two little glands that sit on top of each kidney. I call them your *A batteries*. The adrenal glands help your body deal with stress. They secrete adrenaline in crisis situations to give you extra energy to handle an immediate crisis.

The adrenals are also the key players in the "fight-or-flight" response. Years ago when our population was not so stressed out, this response came in handy when dangerous situations arose, whether it was during battle or running from a lion or tiger. Today we have fallen victim to chronic unrelenting stress coupled with suppressed emotions that are causing a plethora of mind/body-connected symptoms.

When this happens our bodies produce an almost constant stream of adrenaline, which in turn causes us to feel stressed out even more, hyped up and dead tired. When the adrenal glands are in trouble, you must eliminate all lifestyle habits that are destroying the adrenals. By this I mean limit caffeine and sugar, make sure you are sleeping enough and eat healthy foods.

Here are some more symptoms that occur when your A batteries are drained: lethargy, poor memory, moodiness, irritability, hypoglycemia, low immunity, dry skin, brittle nails, sugar cravings, anxiety, weakness, shaky feeling and profound fatigue. The eating plan I have developed for you is perfect for the adrenal glands because it is low in sugar and fats and contains seafood, green super foods and brown rice, which are restoratives for the adrenals. (See page 72.)

Exercise is another way to boost your adrenal health because it releases stress and tension. Just don't overdo it. So many people with anxiety strive for perfection and excellence in all things—sometimes to a fault. In moderation, regular exercise will help diffuse and release your daily stress.

Sleep is crucial. During the night your body has a chance to heal and regenerate. Your nervous system gets a break from the devastating effects of dangerous emotions. Sleep recharges not only the adrenal glands but your entire system as well.

An adrenal glandular supplement will help to nourish and stimulate your exhausted adrenals. It will also help to reduce inflammation and increase body tone and endurance that is so often lost when we are depleted. When vitamins B and C are added or included in the adrenal glandular supplement, the results are even better.

Candida, chronic fatigue syndrome, allergies and blood sugar imbalances such as hypoglycemia and diabetes are greatly improved by taking an adrenal glandular supplement.

CHECK YOUR BATTERIES

If you want to see just how well your adrenal glands are performing, try this self-test. First lie down and rest for five minutes. Then take your blood pressure. Stand up immediately and take your blood pressure reading once more.

If your blood pressure is lower after you stand up, you probably have reduced adrenal gland function, which means your batteries need a charge. The lower the blood pressure reading is from your resting blood pressure, the more severe your low adrenal function is.

The systolic number (or the number on top of the blood pressure reading) normally is about ten points higher when you are standing than when you lie down. A difference of more than ten points should be addressed immediately, for it is extremely important for your journey back to health. Feed your worn-out adrenals the following supplements to bring them back to full power.

1. *Pantothenic acid* is a B vitamin known as an antistress vitamin, which plays a role in the production of adrenal hormones. It is very helpful in alleviating anxiety and depression by fortifying the adrenal glands. In addition, we need pantothenic acid to produce our own natural pain relievers, including cortisol. This is vitally important because pain often goes hand in hand with emotional depletion.

2. *B complex* consists of the full spectrum of B vitamins. B vitamins help to maintain a healthy nervous system.

3. *Vitamin C* is required for tissue growth and repair, healthy gums and adrenal gland function. Vitamin C also protects us against infection and strengthens our immunity.

4. *Royal Jelly* (2 teaspoonfuls daily) is known to be a blessing for the body against asthma, liver disease, skin disorders and immune suppression. This is because it is rich in vitamins, minerals, enzymes and hormones. In addition, it possesses antibiotic and antibacterial properties. It also naturally contains a high concentration of pantothenic acid.

5. *Astragalus* (as directed on the bottle) is a herb that aids adrenal gland function. It also combats fatigue and protects the immune system. This herb played a large part in fortifying and strengthening my body when I battled the Epstein-Barr virus. It is a powerful herb for boosting the immune system.

6. *L-tyrosine* is an amino acid that helps to build the body's natural supply of adrenaline and thyroid hormones. It converts to L-dopa, which makes it a safe therapy for depression. If you are on antidepressants or have cancer, you should avoid tyrosine.

7. *Adrenal Complex Glandular* is a dietary supplement that contains bovine adrenal tissue concentrate, which helps to support and strengthen the adrenal glands.

EIGHT WARNING SIGNS OF ADRENAL EXHAUSTION

The causes of adrenal exhaustion include unrelenting stress, a type A personality and long-term use of corticosteroid drugs for asthma, arthritis and allergies. Too much sugar and caffeine in the diet or deficiencies of vitamins B and C can also contribute to adrenal exhaustion. Adrenal exhaustion is also common during the perimenopausal and menopausal stage of life. Symptoms include:

1. Severe reactions to odors or certain foods
2. Recurring yeast infections
3. Heart palpitations and panic attacks
4. Dry skin and peeling nails
5. Clammy hands and soles of feet
6. Low energy and poor memory
7. Chronic low-back pain
8. Cravings for salt and sugar

PROTOCOL AT A GLANCE

To restore adrenal function and jump-start your batteries, try these things:

1. Rest, rest, rest!
2. Include vitamin C in your daily supplements.
3. Add pantothenic acid to your supplements.
4. Use an adrenal glandular supplement. (Find this at your local health food store.)
5. Add the amino acid tyrosine to your daily supplements.
6. Add foods to your diet that will support good adrenal health. These include brown rice, almonds, garlic, salmon, flounder, lentils, sunflower seeds, bran, brewers yeast and avocado.
7. Begin to use Royal Jelly.

If you are a woman going through menopause, it's crucial that you attend to the health of your adrenal glands for they help to pick up the slack created by your ovaries as their hormone production decreases.

Finding an adrenal glandular supplement with licorice and Siberian ginseng in the same formula is especially beneficial to help stimulate the adrenals to regulate body energy and vibrancy during and after menopause.

HELP FROM THE MIDWEST
CENTER FOR STRESS AND ANXIETY

As I mentioned earlier, I was helped enormously by the tapes and workbook by Lucinda Basset in the Attacking Anxiety Program. This program helped me to understand the mechanics of my panic attacks, longstanding anxiety and strange body symptoms. Let's take a closer look at this powerful program.

Over the past twelve years, over a hundred thousand people have used the skills of the Attacking Anxiety Program. The tape program is an outgrowth of the Midwest Center's Outpatient Clinical Treatment Program for anxiety, panic disorder and agoraphobia. The Midwest Center's staff includes medical doctors, psychologists and psychiatrists. The taped testimonials from those who have contributed their personal experiences offer just as much help.

If you suffer from anxiety, depression or panic attacks, you will definitely recognize yourself many times in this program. The program is cognitive in format, meaning that you will learn how to recognize your behaviors and reactions to stressful situations in your life as well as learn how to change those negative, anxiety-producing behaviors and reactions. You will learn coping strategies to help alleviate your life-disrupting symptoms and calm your fears.

The goal of the program is to teach you to rely on your own skills for recovery. This tape program is very effective for a broad range of anxiety disorders because all anxiety disorders are addressed in much the same way. This program provides:

- A complete understanding of the cause and effect
- Comprehension and implementation of proven coping skills, including exposure to your fears and concerns

Lucinda Bassett feels that if even one of the above elements is missing in the approach to anxiety, complete recovery is impossible. I agree; knowledge is power! Anxiety affects your peace of mind and quality of life, your ability to make decisions and commitments, your family and your relationships. When you are set free from anxiety once and for all, you won't worry constantly about your health, sanity and life.[2]

STRESS BUSTERS FROM NATURE

Following is a list of stress-busting herbs that can make all the difference in your battle against anxiety.[3]

SIBERIAN GINSENG

Siberian ginseng is a root that belongs to the ginseng family of adaptogenic herbs. Adaptogens help build our resistance to stress. Siberian ginseng helps the body adapt to stress and reduces fatigue, often the underlying factors in the anxiety picture. It improves oxygen and blood sugar metabolism as well as immune function.

In 1977, one thousand stressed workers in the Soviet Union took Siberian ginseng and realized improved health and stamina. They reported 40 percent fewer sick days, and the workers saw 50 percent fewer illnesses overall. Pretty impressive!

The recommended dosage is 180 to 360 milligrams of Siberian ginseng extract standardized to 0.8 percent eleutherosides, in two equally divided doses. Take daily for two to three months, then take a two-week break before resuming.

Siberian ginseng is a stimulant, so don't take it before bed or if you have high blood pressure. It's not for severe anxiety. See your doctor if your symptoms are severe.

One last tip, do not confuse Siberian ginseng with Panax ginseng. The Panax version can increase your body's cortisol—and cortisol is your body's stress hormone.

VALERIAN

Valerian is widely used in Europe as a sedative. The Chinese use it also to treat nervous conditions and insomnia. Its effect is said to be similar to benzodiazepine tranquilizers but without side effects. Valerian works like benzodiazepines by enhancing the activity of GABA. The dosage is 300 to 900 milligrams of valerian extract (standardized to 0.8 percent valeric acid) taken one hour before bedtime for insomnia. Also 50 to 100 milligrams taken two to three times a day may help relieve performance anxiety and stress. Do not take valerian with alcohol. Side effects are rare but may include headache and stimulant effects in some people. The effects of valerian use are cumulative, so you have to take it for two to three weeks before evaluating your results. I call valerian *God's sleeping pill!*

PASSIONFLOWER

Passionflower is a climbing plant, native to North America. Passionflower combined with valerian is a popular herbal remedy throughout much of Europe for insomnia, anxiety and irritability.

ST. JOHN'S WORT

St. John's wort has been used to treat anxiety and depression in Europe for twenty-four hundred years. Pretty impressive, wouldn't you say? Once again, here is a natural substance that enhances the activity of GABA. In addition, St. John's wort enhances the activity of three important neurotransmitters—serotonin, norepinephrine and dopamine. In a study published in the *British Medical Journal* in 1996, based on 1,008 patients, St. John's wort proved to be an effective treatment for mild to moderately severe depression with almost zero side effects. The standardized dose is 300 milligrams extract (standardized to 0.3 percent hypericin) three times per day. St. John's wort must be taken for six weeks before evaluating your results, because the effect is cumulative and not immediate. Do not take St. John's wort if you are currently taking prescription anti-depressants, especially MAO inhibitors (Nardil, Parnate). If you stop taking a prescription antidepressant, wait at least four weeks before taking St. John's wort to make sure that no overlapping occurs. Side effects are very rare but include dizziness and gastrointestinal irritation.

KAVA

Comes from the root of piper methysticum, a member of the pepper tree family native to the South Pacific. Kava is proven for both short-term and long-term treatment. Anxiety, tension, fear and insomnia decreased steadily in a 1997 randomized placebo-controlled study in which 101 outpatients took 70 milligrams of kavalactones or a placebo.[4]

Kava has a natural tranquilizing effect on the brain by producing a soothing effect in the amygdala, the brain's alarm center. The recommended dosage is 70 to 85 milligrams (70 percent kavalactones), taken in the evening. You may increase the dose to as much as 100 milligrams three times daily if necessary.

Do not mix kava with alcohol, pharmaceutical antidepressants, benzodiazepine, tranquilizers or sleeping pills. If you have Parkinson's disease, kava may worsen muscular weakness. Extremely high doses of kava (ten times the normal dose) can cause vision, breathing and muscle problems. Yellowing and scaly skin has also occurred at high doses. Kava, if used properly, can bring blessed relief.[5]

5-HTP

5-HTP is derived from the seed of the griffonia tree and is related to the amino acid tryptophan. It is used to treat anxiety, insomnia, depression and other related conditions linked with low levels of serotonin. 5-HTP is a raw material the body uses to manufacture serotonin, the neurotransmitter linked to mood. By raising serotonin levels in the body, anxiety and depression can be relieved. Informal studies suggest that 5-HTP is effective for mild, moderate anxiety and full-blown anxiety disorders.

The most effective study dose range was 75–100 milligrams per day. You should start with 25 milligrams per day at the time of the day when you feel most anxious.[6]

WHICH WAY TO GO—DRUGS OR HERBS?

Ultimately you must decide which way you will go. Talk to your physician before discontinuing any prescription medication. The following chart serves as a general guideline.

DRUGS OR HERBS?

FOR MODERATE TO SEVERE ANXIETY AND CHRONIC STRESS

PRESCRIPTION DRUGS

- Xanax
- Klonopin
- Tranxene
- Sleeping pills (Restoril, Dalmane, Halcion, Serax)
- Valium
- Ativan

HERBAL ALTERNATIVES

- Kava
- Siberian ginseng as an adaptogen
- Valerian

COST COMPARISON PER MONTH

- Prescription drugs: Benzodiazepines, $15–$20
- Herbal alternatives: Kava, $10–20; valerian, $6–20; Siberian ginseng, $8–24

FOR DEPRESSION AND ANXIETY

PRESCRIPTION DRUGS (SSRIs)

- Paxil
- Zoloft
- Prozac

Side effects: Weight gain, sexual dysfunction, insomnia, nausea, nervousness, agitation, heart palpitations, sweating

HERBAL ALTERNATIVES

- St. John's wort
- 5-HTP

COST COMPARISON PER MONTH

- Prescription drugs: SSRIs, $70–$80
- Herbal alternatives: St. John's wort, $8–15; 5-HTP, $11–50

SUGAR SABOTAGE

Do you reach for sugar in times of stress, depression and anxiety? ⌐ is especially detrimental to your brain and body function. 'tion, excessive sugar consumption suppresses your body's immune response. If you are consuming too much sugar on a daily basis, you may be setting yourself up for low blood sugar. Many people who suffer from anxiety and depression also have to deal with hypoglycemia. Notice how the symptoms of anxiety are identical to the following profile of a hypoglycemic individual:

- Rapid pulse
- Heart palpitations
- Cold sweats
- Fatigue
- Twitching
- Crying spells
- Weakness
- Irritability
- Nightmares
- Poor concentration

If these symptoms are familiar to you, you must focus on eating more fiber and protein foods at each meal and cut back on simple sugar. It is very important that you have a protein snack between meals. This will keep your blood sugar levels stable all day long. It is true that limiting or even eliminating sugar will not be easy. But to rebuild your brain and body, sugar consumption must be curtailed. The following dietary supplements will help you make the adjustment.

- Chromium picolinate
- B complex
- Vitamin C
- Pantothenic acid
- Adrenal gland supplement
- Calcium and magnesium
- A protein shake each morning
- Stevia extract, used as a sugar-balancing herbal sweetener
- Add fiber to your diet (brown rice, for example)

It is wise to balance your blood sugar now because low blood sugar can predispose you to developing diabetes later on in life. Diabetes occurs when all of the sugar and carbohydrates that a person consumes are not used properly. Sooner or later the pancreas no longer produces insulin, creating high blood sugar. This can be very dangerous.

According to the U. S. Department of Health and Human Services, more than twenty million people suffer from diabetes in this country.[7] Diabetes can lead to heart and kidney disease, stroke, blindness, hypertension and even death.

Take this short quiz to see if your sugar consumption may not only be affecting your level of health now, but later on as well.

IS SUGAR AFFECTING YOUR HEALTH?

Yes   No

❑   ❑   Do you have a family history of diabetes?

❑   ❑   Do you crave sweets at certain times of the day?

❑   ❑   When under stress, do you crave sweets?

❑   ❑   Do you consume ice cream, chocolate, pies, cakes and candy more than twice a week?

❑   ❑   Do you feel weak and shaky if your meal is delayed?

❑   ❑   Do you feel tense, uptight and nervous at certain times during the day?

❑   ❑   Do you crave sodas or other sweetened soft drinks?

❑   ❑   Do you pay attention to low-fat foods while ignoring the higher sugar content typically found in them?

Studies have shown that people suffering from depression had fewer symptoms when sugar was removed from their diets. In addition, excessive sugar consumption leads to:

• High cholesterol and triglycerides and the risk of atherosclerosis
• Excessive emotional swings and food cravings, especially before menstruation
• Tooth decay and gum loss

Even small blood sugar fluctuations disturb a person's sense of well-being. Large fluctuations caused by consuming too much sugar cause feelings of depression, anxiety, mood swings, fatigue and even aggressive behavior.

By combining low glycemic foods, such as fiber foods, together with exercise, amino acid supplementation and nutritional supplements that help balance your blood sugar, you can optimize your brain's biochemistry.

No sugar? But how?

Your eating plan has blood sugar balance in mind. In addition, I always include chromium picolinate, 200 micrograms if you weigh one hundred fifty pounds. If you weigh more than one hundred fifty pounds, add another 200 micrograms for a total of 400 micrograms in divided doses.

Chromium will help you as you wean yourself off simple sugars that have been robbing you of your health. You'll be interested to know that people who consume too much simple sugar and who are under constant stress are typically low in chromium. Often I have seen my clients experience a heightened sense of well-being after following this eating plan and taking chromium picolinate. I have also found that chromium increases energy levels. I believe this is because of the blood sugar balancing effect on the body. The energy peaks and valleys disappear and are replaced with an even, sustained energy.

In addition to chromium, I recommend pantothenic acid, which is a B vitamin that helps the body handle stress. This vitamin does wonders for your adrenal glands, which are so often zapped by caffeine, sugar, lack of sleep and stress.

Pantothenic acid and chromium picolinate will help you make the lifestyle changes you need to experience a balanced mind and body. Instead of sugar, I personally use Stevia extract to sweeten my tea or anything that requires sweetening. You will find that this noncaloric sweetener is a wonderful blessing, and it's safe for diabetics and hypoglycemics.

Why eliminate artificial sweeteners?

America has jumped on the artificial sweetener bandwagon because of our obsession and preoccupation with our weight. This seems like a simple answer for those trying to watch their sugar calories. Did you know that one of the components of aspartame is methanol? Methanol is considered toxic even in small amounts. You will be interested to know that methanol is also known as wood alcohol. Why would you even consider putting this into your body? In addition, toxic levels of methanol have been associated with

59

brain swelling, inflammation of the heart muscle and pancreas and even blindness! It has also been blamed for convulsions, memory loss, mood swings, headaches, nausea and more.

Eat as close to the original garden as possible. This means eating natural foods or foods that are close to their original form. Aspartame is made synthetically. It's also implicated in fetal brain damage. Therefore, pregnant and lactating women and very young or allergy-prone children should avoid aspartame.

Natural whole-food sweeteners are available that can satisfy your occasional sweet tooth without the health risks. The natural sweeteners that are allowed on this emotional recovery program are:

- *Honey*—twice as sweet as sugar. Avoid if you are diabetic or have candida or low blood sugar. It contains vitamins and enzymes.
- *Rice syrup*—40 percent as sweet as sugar, made from rice and water.
- *Sucarat*—natural sweetener made from sugar cane juice. A concentrated sweetener that should be used with caution if you have blood sugar imbalance.
- *Stevia herb*—herb from South America that can be used in beverages, baking and cooking. Safe for persons with blood sugar imbalances and/or candida and diabetes. Stevia comes in two forms: liquid extract or white powered extract. Stevia is my personal favorite!
- *Fructose*—twice as sweet as sugar. Derived from fruit. Not allowed if you have candida.

PERSONALITY PERILS OF SUGAR[8]

Here are the mental and emotional signs of too much sugar:

- Chronic or frequent bouts of depression with manic depressive tendencies
- Difficulty concentrating, forgetfulness or absentmindedness
- Lack of motivation, loss of enthusiasm for plans and projects

- Becoming increasingly undependable, inconsistent thoughts and actions
- Moody personality changes with emotional outbursts
- Irritability, mood swings

These brain and body symptoms are associated with excess sugar consumption:

- Anxiety and panic attacks
- Bulimia
- Candidiasis, chronic fatigue syndrome
- Diabetes or hypoglycemia
- Food addiction with loss of B vitamins and minerals
- Obesity
- Menopausal mood swings and unusual low energy

BRAIN BALANCE AT A GLANCE

(Please refer to the back of this book for a complete listing of products and where they can be purchased.)

1. To help calm your mind try:
   - Bach Rescue Remedy (refer to page 93)
   - Kava kava
   - Passionflower

2. Adaptogens to strengthen the body in times of stress
   - Siberian ginseng
   - Astragalus
   - Suma
   - Jiaogulan

3. Feed your adrenal glands
   - Core Level Adrenal
   - Pantothenic acid
   - Royal Jelly
   - B-complex vitamins
   - Have a green drink daily (Kyo-Green or liquid chlorophyll)

4. Nerve food
   - Gotu kola
   - Gingko biloba
   - Vitamin C
   - Niacinamide

5. Amino ammo
   - GABA–capsules
   - Brain Link–amino acid powder
   - SAMe–400 milligrams daily

6. Mind minerals
   - Calcium
   - Magnesium

7. Fatty acids are essential
   - Evening primrose oil
   - Flax oil

SLEEP DEEP WITHOUT DRUGS

Our mind and body pay the price when we shortchange ourselves by as little as an hour's sleep each day. Following are five ways to insure that your sleep is restful and restoring.

1. *Avoid alcohol and other stimulants.* As the body breaks down alcohol, its sedative properties give way to arousing ones, jolting us awake during REM (rapid eye movement) sleep. Caffeine is also out for the obvious fact that it is a stimulant.

2. *Take a hot bath.* A hot bath before bedtime helps people fall asleep as well as Ambien, a leading prescription sleeping pill, according to Cynthia Dorsey, PhD, director of the Sleep Health Center, which is affiliated with McLean Hospital in Bedford.

3. *"Got milk?"* Grandma was right! Tryptophan, an amino acid found in milk, is a building block of serotonin, a

neurotransmitter that helps bring on sleep. This is true whether you warm the milk or not.

4. *Maintain a routine.* People who rise and retire at the same time every day are less likely to experience insomnia or to complain about daytime fatigue.

5. *Don't be a clock watcher.* Turn your clock toward the wall. Compulsive clock watching will only keep you awake.[9]

While writing this book I came across an interesting article titled "The Brain's Balancing Act" that was very informative. In essence the article said that working either the left or right side of your brain too hard can wreak havoc with your entire body. By stimulating the underused portion of your brain, balance can be restored. When your brain is in balance, your well-being increases, netting immediate health benefits.[10]

Let's examine this theory. The left side of our brain sees individual parts that make up a whole. It organizes, analyzes and rationalizes information. It is also the verbal side of your brain, responding to speech and using words to name and describe things. It also keeps track of time and thinks in terms of consequences. The right brain addresses emotions and is affected by music, touch and body language. It follows hunches and feelings rather than logic. It is the visual side of your brain responding to pictures, colors and shapes. Overreliance on one side can create frustration and eventual brain burnout. As you have learned, what affects the brain also affects the body. So, the effects of brain burnout can lead to physical problems such as insomnia, headaches and fatigue. This is because a body cannot be healthy if the brain is not in balance.[11]

I have included a chart developed by Ann McCombs, DO, who works with hemispericity. She has found that certain symptoms indicate a brain imbalance. Most symptoms are left- or right-side specific. There are, however, some signs that could indicate a strain of either side.

DON'T OVERTAX YOUR BRAIN

Signs that the right brain is overtaxed

- Staring off into space
- Feelings of panic
- Difficulty paying attention
- Feeling overly sensitive and emotional

For right brain relief

- Work on a crossword puzzle
- Organize your closet
- Play a game of logic (chess)
- Learn new software
- Develop a personal budget

Signs that the left brain is overtaxed

- Feelings of worry
- Difficulty communicating
- Inability to follow a schedule
- Difficult problem solving

For left brain relief

- Dance
- Listen to music
- Cook or make a gourmet dish
- Play with your children
- Take a walk outdoors

By stimulating the under-used side of your brain, balance occurs, and your brain drain goes right down the drain.

KEEP YOUR BRAIN BOOSTED

Lovable lecithin

Lecithin benefits the brain and the body. One of the easiest ways to enhance the health of your brain, nervous system, cardiovascular system, liver and other vital parts of your body is to supplement your body with lecithin. It has been said that lecithin does more to improve and preserve our health than any other nutrient.

Lecithin is found in virtually every cell of our body and is most concentrated in our liver, kidneys and brain. I recommend lecithin to people with high blood lipids and high total cholesterol since lecithin helps to dissolve fats and cholesterol by acting as an emulsifier. They have gotten great results and now make it a part of their daily protocol.

Do you need to supplement your body with a daily dose of lecithin? I'll let you be the judge. The following information will help you make a quick decision about this nutrient.

Scientific studies show that we can repress or minimize age-related changes in our brain such as memory loss associated with aging through the long-term use of a lecithin supplement. This is very exciting for older persons and those who battle higher-than-normal cholesterol. Dietary sources of lecithin, in the amounts needed to be therapeutic and effective, are very few. That's why I recommend supplementation with lecithin granules.

In your liver, lecithin metabolizes clogging fat, thereby reducing the chance of liver degeneration. In your bloodstream, as mentioned earlier, lecithin prevents cholesterol fats from accumulating on the walls of your arteries and can help to dissolve deposits that may already be there. Lecithin helps your intestinal tract to absorb vitamins and other nutrients. In addition, lecithin benefits the nervous system, skin and distribution of body fat. I personally take lecithin for the fat-emulsifying and brain tonic properties. There is a family history of high cholesterol and heart disease in my family, so I make sure to take my lecithin daily. Two teaspoons daily may be added to food or juice.

Lecithin is derived from soybeans and egg yolk. Food sources of lecithin include grains, legumes, fish, wheat germ and brewers yeast. I use lecithin granules derived from soybean. People who are battling serious diseases such as chronic fatigue syndrome and other immune disorders may benefit more from egg yolk lecithin. With this in mind, use soy lecithin for brain and cholesterol concerns and egg yolk lecithin for immune disorder conditions. For your convenience I have listed my source for soy lecithin at the back of the book. I feel that this is the best tasting with 95 percent phosphatides, high quality from soy.[12]

ADDITIONAL BRAIN BOOSTING

When you are under stress your brain needs constant attention to keep your mental edge. Make sure that you feed it all the nutrients it needs to function at optimal levels. By taking care of your brain now, you will safeguard yourself from the consequences of aging.

Over time, your brain doesn't produce as many neurotransmitters as it once did. So supplementation becomes very important when you experience stress and when you begin to age. This is where gingko can be of help in the battle against mental decline. Gingko enhances neurotransmitter production and helps your brain use glucose for energy production. Another bonus is that gingko improves the flow of blood through the brain's tiny capillaries, which in turn increases the brain's supply of oxygen and glucose. Gingko can help offset ordinary memory loss over a three-month period. Tinnitus (ringing in the ears) also has been helped or alleviated by using gingko. It is not recommended, however, if you are on blood thinners of any kind because it may enhance their effect.

B ON THE BRAIN

Since this book is devoted to emotional stress, I would be remiss if I did not discuss the importance of the B vitamins. Proper functioning of the nervous system is dramatically affected by B vitamins. I believe that B vitamins are the most influential factor in maintaining a healthy nervous system. When my clients are under stress of any kind, whether it be physical, emotional or mental, I recommend a good total B complex post haste. As you read on, you'll see why the B vitamins are my favorite in time of stress.

B_1, commonly known as thiamine, is also known as the "morale vitamin" because of its beneficial effect on mental attitude. It is also crucial to the health of the nervous system. If your diet is high in carbohydrates, then B_1 is absolutely essential. B_1 also improves food assimilation, thereby stabilizing your appetite.

Here are some symptoms of B_1 deficiency: fatigue, loss of ankle and knee reflexes, mental instability, forgetfulness, fears, cardiac malfunctions such as rapid rhythm and palpitations and inflammation of the optic nerve.

B_2, which is known as riboflavin, is a water-soluble vitamin that is easily absorbed through the small intestines. It plays an important part in any chemical reactions in the body. B_2 deficiency symptoms are as follows: shiny tongue, eye burning and itching, feeling of sand or grit in eyes, oily skin, difficulty in urination and scaling around mouth, nose and ears. B_2 has been shown to also be an inhibitor of tumor growth.

B_6 may have the greatest effect on the immune system of all the B vitamins, because a deficiency can result in a vast array of problems in the immune response. A lack of B_6 will decrease the size of the thymus, the gland that produces T-cells. A B_6 deficiency is also linked to tumor growth.

B_{12} is a B vitamin that neither man nor animal can manufacture in their bodies. Also known as cobalamin, it is the most complex of all the B group molecularly. B_{12} is needed in the body for the formation of red blood cells. B_{12} must be combined with calcium for proper absorption. This powerful vitamin has a stimulating effect on the immune system. When deficient, anemia can occur along with sore tongue, weight loss, mental deterioration, menstrual disturbances and "needles and pins" sensation.

Vitamin B_{12} is crucial because this vitamin helps the body properly process fats. Vitamin B_{12} is also used to form oxygen-carrying red blood cells, which are needed to prevent mentally distracting fatigue and low energy. Many people have a hard time absorbing B_{12} from the foods that they eat, and vegetarian foods are lacking in this important vitamin, so I recommend that everyone take a B-complex vitamin that contains B_{12}.

Pantothenic acid, or B_5, is a blessing when a person is under stress. It remains my favorite even now. It has an enhancing and beneficial effect upon the adrenal glands where proper functioning is crucial during times of stressful conditions. With this information in mind, be sure to take your Bs.

Exercise is another lesson in body/mind connection. A fit body contributes to a fit mind. Exercise keeps your blood well supplied with oxygen by increasing your lung capacity and conditioning your heart. This will super-charge your brain. Exercise also causes the brain to produce nerve growth factor, or NGF. It is nerve growth factor, that helps brain cells to create branches that connect to fellow brain cells, speeding the transfer of information. Any type of exercise performed at least three times a week should prove helpful.

WHEN IT'S GOOD TO HAVE A FAT HEAD

A Harvard study showed that Omega-3 fatty acids can help reduce bad moods. Additional studies point out that taking Omega-3 fats can improve scores on psychological tests.[13]

The typical American diet does not supply the proper essential fatty acids (EFAs) on its own. It is important for you to supplement your diet because EFAs not only help brain function, but cardiovascular, nervous system, fat metabolism, skin health and joint flexibility as well. They're not called essential fatty acids for nothing. Look for a EFA formula with Omega-3 and Omega-6 oils derived from fish oil, flax oil or borage oil.

My personal favorites are:

- For Omega 3—Carlson Salmon Oil (liquid or capsules)
- Combination Omega-3 and Omega-6—Nature's Secret Ultimate Oil, Wakanaga's Kyolic EPA

Please note that even though you will find most of these fatty acids in dark containers to keep out light, keep them in the refrigerator and use them quickly because they can go rancid. If you cannot use a bottle of oil in a month, then purchase a smaller bottle or stick with capsules. This is especially true for flaxseed oil. I keep my Nature's Secret Ultimate Oil or Kyolic EPA in my refrigerator even though it's not imperative that you do so.

OTHER BRAIN HELPERS

- *Phosphatidyl serine (PS)* helps to transmit nerve impulses from one cell to another. It has been found to be useful in various types of memory loss.

- *Acetyl-L-carnitine (ALC)* helps to ease depression and helps cells burn fat for energy and fight free radicals.
- *Huperzine A* is derived from Chinese moss, and it helps the brain hang on to acetylcholine, which is a neurotransmitter vital to memory. A Chinese study found that huperzine A improved the mental functioning of Alzheimer's patients.

Put this information into your brain's memory bank along with the recommended brain boosters, add in regular exercise, and you will be well on the way to making the most of your mind now and in the future.[14]

CHAPTER 5

Steps to a Healthy Brain

solation may make you more likely to fall victim to Alzheimer's or related brain conditions.[1] It is important to stay socially involved by joining a church, volunteering or traveling. It is also important to keep your brain sharp by doing mind-exercising activities like cross word puzzles, games such as Trivial Pursuit, reading and memorizing passages.

STAY CONNECTED

Good or bad, your feelings need expression; they must be recognized and given the freedom to reveal themselves.

Don't hide behind a smile when your heart is breaking. Let your feelings out and release your pain. Give it to God. He will help you to then reconstruct your life and enjoy the things that bring joy to your life once again.

Please remember, you are on a very personal journey into emotional wellness and physical health. At times you may expect the answers to come quickly, but try to be patient. Some answers can take a lifetime to be revealed to you. You are embarking on the important journey of discovering who you are and what gifts you have to offer. Celebrate, for there is happiness awaiting you.

SELF-ESTEEM—IT'S A GOOD THING

In October 1982 George Gallop Jr. of the Gallop Poll reported to Dr. Robert Schuller the results of a nationwide poll on self-esteem.

CHECK YOUR SELF-ESTEEM

People with high esteem had these eight things in common:

- They have a close relationship with God.
- They are morally sensitive.
- They are greater work producers.
- They consider success in human values rather than monetary values.
- They have strong family relationships.
- They are more generous and more charitable.
- They have fewer health problems.
- They have fewer stress-related problems than the general public.

THE OCEAN OF EMOTION

- Every day, each minute is no longer a struggle. I have let go, and my mind, body and spirit are free.
- I can sit in peaceful silence and focus on my breathing.
- I am no longer distracted; my body is working with me, not against me.
- My body and mind are experiencing serenity I have never known before. I have developed an inner strength that carries me through the most difficult of times.
- The ocean of emotion is not drowning me; I am flowing with the current, not against it.

FOOD FOR THE BODY—THE EATING PLAN

Dangerous emotions can lead to obesity. When you are angry, irritable, resentful, unforgiving and uptight, your levels of the stress hormone called *cortisol* become elevated. Cortisol stimulates your appetite because one of its main roles in the stress response is to refuel you with carbohydrates and fats after you have completed the fight-or-flight response. Here's the catch: If you never complete the fight-or-flight response and leave your stress-response motor running from unresolved dangerous emotions, the result will be an insatiable appetite for sweets—the quick fix for stress relief.

72

This quick fix leads to a quick expansion of your waistline.

Now for the good news: Only 30 percent of our stress responses are genetic. That means that 70 percent are environmental. So it follows that if you learn to identify and release the things that are stressing you, you will be able to cut the dangerous emotional connection to obesity off at the pass. Remember, don't sweat the small stuff—and everything is small stuff. When you replenish your brain, renew the mind and rebuild the body, you will come into balance. When you are balanced, you are more able to control your cravings because your cortisol levels will not be elevated. You will be able to practice "nutritious noshing," meaning snacking on nutrient-dense foods that build your health without piling on the pounds. Here are some tips for controlling cortisol calories.

1. Exercise to get your endorphins pumping. This will neutralize stress hormones.
2. Know your panic buttons. Diffuse your dangerous emotions. Just ask yourself, *Is it worth sacrificing my health over?*
3. Have a protein shake when you are feeling stressed. Protein demands go up during stressful periods. Remember, amino acids are the building blocks of protein. Amino acids are crucial for brain health.

Many people who are struggling with emotional pain fail to care for themselves. It is bad enough to feel emotionally drained. But when you add in the neglect of your body, physical breakdown and illness are not far away. The following eating plan has proved to be a godsend during times of stress, illness and when your health needs to be taken to a higher level. In other words, it's good all of the time.

It is important to make a conscious effort to eat properly, for the body needs high-quality fuel to repair, rebuild and regenerate. This eating plan is high in nutrition, yet it eliminates all the foods that can lower the immune response (white sugar, white flour, dairy, wheat and yeast) during times of stress. In addition, there is emphasis on blood sugar balancing.

THE EATING PLAN

ON RISING

8-ounce glass of water with ½ fresh lemon to clean kidneys–add
Stevia extract to sweeten
Add 1 teaspoon of apple cider vinegar if there is flatulence

BREAKFAST

1 or 2 poached or hard-boiled eggs on a slice of millet bread
OR oatmeal with 1 tablespoon Bragg's Aminos (Refer to page 75.)
You may also have oatbran
OR buckwheat pancakes with a little butter or almond butter
OR almond butter on millet toast

MIDMORNING

Have a green drink (liquid chlorophyll or Kyo-Green)
OR a cup of dandelion tea
OR a small bottle of water

LUNCH

A fresh green salad with lemon and olive oil dressing
OR an open-face millet sandwich with mayonnaise, veggies, seafood,
turkey or chicken
OR a vegetable soup with a piece of millet bread
OR chicken, tuna or vegetable pasta salad

MIDAFTERNOON

Rice crackers or baked corn chips with some rice cheese or soy cheese
OR a bottled water with a hard-boiled or deviled egg
OR raw veggies (if tolerated)
ALSO, cup of green tea, with Stevia to sweeten

DINNER

Baked, broiled or poached fish or chicken or turkey with steamed brown
rice
OR baked potato with Bragg's Aminos, or a little rice or soy cheese
OR an oriental stir-fry with brown rice and Bragg's Aminos
OR a small omelet with a veggie filling (soy or rice cheese can be added)
OR a vegetarian casserole
OR a hot or cold vegetable pasta salad

BEFORE BED

Cup of herb tea such as dandelion or chamomile with Stevia to sweeten
and balance blood sugar

RECOMMENDED SUPPLEMENTS

Here's a list of the supplements I've mentioned. These
supplements are available at your local health food store.

1. *Kyo-Green*—a complete green super food that contains protein and all the B vitamins. It heals the intestinal tract, strengthens the liver and boosts immune health. It is a good detoxifier and blood cleanser rich in chlorophyll.

2. *Stevia Extract*—for blood sugar balance and anti-fungal properties. This product is designed to aid in blood sugar balance. Stevia is twenty-five times sweeter than sugar and balances the blood sugar. It also has zero calories. Make a delicious lemonade with fresh lemons, water and Stevia extract. Drink it throughout the day. It tastes great and helps keep blood sugar stable—enjoy! *Stevia rebaudiana,* also known as "sweet herb," is a South American sweetening leaf. Health-related benefits include those associated with regulating blood sugar, lowering blood pressure and even preventing tooth decay.

3. *Bragg's Amino Acids*—a natural health alternative to soy sauce made from soybean and purified water. Spray or dash of liquid aminos for salads and dressings, soups, veggies, rice and beans, tofu, wok and stir-fries, macrobiotics, casseroles, potatoes, meats, fish, poultry, jerky, tempeh, gravies, sauces and popcorn (no chemicals, no alcohol, no additives, no preservatives).

YOUR "MANTLE" FOR STRESS RELIEF

Between 60 and 90 percent of all medical office visits in the United States are for stress-related disorders, according to The Mind/ Body Medical Institute at Harvard Medical School.[2]

Mind/body medicine, or the use of relaxation techniques to fight stress-related illnesses, could be one of the most important medical treatments of the twenty-first century. Dr. Gregg D. Jacobs, an assistant professor of psychiatry at Harvard Medical School and a senior scientist with the Mind/Body Institute, discussed at the Medicine in the Millennium Conference that there is a proven link between thoughts and emotions and the health of the body.

Mind/body medicine is based on thousands of studies over the past twenty-five years and is now considered mainstream medicine. Practicing the relaxation response makes your cells that fight disease more effective. The relaxation response involves changing your thoughts, which in turn lowers your body's metabolism, heart rate, breathing rate and blood pressure. The relaxation response can be achieved through progressive muscle relaxation, focused breathing, music or prayer.

Jacobs went on to say that mind/body medicine is cost effective with little or no side effects, and the techniques can be taught through books or tapes. Practicing it has been shown to improve a person's sense of well-being.

Here's my own version of relaxation therapy: I have found in my own life when faced with stress and tension that my muscles tighten all over my body and I generally feel miserable. I researched muscle tension and found that physical and emotional stress gets stored in your muscles, making you even more tense. Fortunately there are solutions when you feel yourself tightening up.

Massage therapy has a long history of therapeutic benefits. A stressed body responds beautifully to regular massage therapy sessions. If this sounds a bit impractical for you, don't worry, there's always exercise such as walking, stretching and light weightlifting. But I want to share with you a wonderful technique that will work for you time and time again when you're faced with tight, stressed muscles. I call it the "MANTLE technique."

What is it? It's very simple. My MANTLE technique is simply tensing and holding for the count of ten each part of your body one section at a time. To remind myself that I need attention daily I coined the word MANTLE.

M—MUSCLES
A—ALWAYS
N—NEED
T—TENSION
L—LOOSENING
E—EVERY DAY

That's right! Muscles always need tension loosening–every day. Just begin with your eyes; tense and hold for ten seconds, then release. Take a deep cleansing breath. Try to belly breathe. Fill your diaphragm with air and exhale slowly through your mouth. Next, tighten all of the muscles of your face and mouth, make a face and hold it for ten seconds. Take another deep cleansing breath, continue this tensing and releasing exercise on down to the other parts of your body. This would include your neck, shoulders, arms, hands, fingers, stomach, lower abdomen, upper thighs, calves, feet and toes. After each area has been relaxed, use the time to give thanks to God for all of the wonderful blessings He has bestowed upon you.

QUICK RELAXER

Massaging is another powerful tool to help you learn to beat the effects of stress.

Self massage–To ease your neck muscles, place your thumbs at the base of your skull just below your ears. Press inward and upward for six seconds, then release. Repeat, moving your thumbs a quarter inch inward along the base of your skull each time.

To reach your lower back, put four tennis balls in a sock. Place the sock at the base of your back, lie down and roll gently for a few minutes. Your body weight applies the pressure.

To relax your shoulders, place your finger tips on your shoulders at the base of your neck. Press down; hold the pressure for six seconds, release, then repeat gradually, working your fingers down your shoulder line.

EIGHT STRESS BUSTERS

A certain level of stress is not only normal but is an expected part of life. Only when stress is severe, long lasting or happens frequently will our health be jeopardized. Here are eight powerful stress busters to help you create a foundation of good health:

1. *Eat well.* Eating right will keep you well enough to face distressing challenges.

2. *Sleep deeply.* Sleeping soundly is essential for a continually healthy immune system.

3. *Confide in a friend.* In times of great stress you need to be able to talk about your problems and discuss the details with someone you trust who is concerned about you.

4. *Express yourself.* Psychologists recognize that verbalizing your problems is an effective tool for releasing the tensions created by those concerns.

5. *Get physical.* The movement of blood increases general immune protection and at the same time helps buffer the immunosuppression of distress. Regular exercise is a natural release for the body's response to stress.

6. *Make time to unwind.* Set aside a period of time every day to relax and listen to music. Take a warm bath. Take up a hobby. Take a private walk or practice deep breathing. Pick an activity that makes you feel refreshed, renewed and rejuvenated.

7. *Remain clear-headed.* Alcohol or drugs will not cure distress. Your immune system is already suppressed by stress and becomes much more so by alcohol or drug use.

8. *Pray.* Give your cares and worries to the Lord.

DON'T HAVE A BREAKDOWN, HAVE A BREAKTHROUGH!

The goal of this book is to help you recognize just how much your emotional health contributes to the health of your body, mind and spirit. Let it serve as a wake-up call if you are just now beginning to experience stress and anxiety. If you are struggling with full-blown anxiety or depression, let it be a source of information and help, and a blueprint for a restoration of your body, mind and spirit.[3]

WHAT IS YOUR ANXIETY LEVEL?

To get a ballpark idea of how much anxiety you are currently dealing with on a daily basis, take this life situation test.[4]

0 = No anxiety	2 = Moderate anxiety
1 = Mild anxiety	3 = Severe anxiety

SITUATIONAL ANXIETY
_____ Going to a dentist or doctor
_____ Being in a crowd
_____ Waiting in line
_____ Being in an elevator
_____ Flying
_____ Rejection in love or at work
_____ Socializing at a party
_____ Bills
_____ Deadlines
_____ Major purchase or investment
_____ Driving
_____ TOTAL

The higher your score, the more you should follow the guidelines outlined for you in this book. Relief does not come overnight, but just realizing that anxiety can play a huge factor in your overall quality of life can in itself be healing!

Some anxiety is normal and healthy. Use anxiety as a source of information about your lifestyle and your health. Stop and look at it closely; listen to its initial gentle whispers and pay attention. If you turn a deaf ear to it for too long, you could be hit over the head with chronic physical illness. However, if you address the causes of your anxiety early, you may prevent long-term illness. Use your anxiety symptoms as a source of breakthrough, or you could be headed for a breakdown.

> Emotions are the connections between the mind and the body, and there is no separation between the two.
> —CANDACE PERT, PhD

The longer you allow fear to control your behavior, the more predisposed you become to a disease oriented lifestyle. Your ability to handle stress and anxiety depends on your state of health. Your state of health depends on your state of nutrition. Your state of nutrition depends on a well planned program of amino acids, vitamins, and minerals to nourish your brain and body.[5]

STOP AND SMELL THE ROSES

One powerful way to treat anxiety before it attacks your body is through aromatherapy. Aromatherapy is a safe, pleasant way to lift your mood and relieve stress. Your brain perceives smell more rapidly than it does any of your other four senses. When you smell something, the information is relayed directly to the hypothalamus where your motivations, moods, emotions and creativity all begin. The aroma of essential oil molecules works through hormone-like chemicals to produce results. Scents and odors influence the glands responsible for hormone levels, metabolism, insulin and stress levels, appetite, body temperature and even sex drive.

Actual studies of brain waves show that scents such as lavender increase alpha brain waves that are associated with relaxation. Scents such as jasmine boost beta waves that are linked to alertness. Essential oils are most often used to counteract stress and its effects upon the mind and emotions. Essential oils used in aromatherapy calm, sedate and uplift the body, mind and spirit.

Aromatherapy can help to prevent panic attacks. I personally can attest to this. Listed below are essential oils that will help your body, mind and spirit as you continue on your journey to total wellness.

AROMATHERAPY FOR STRESS

- *Lavender* balances your nerves and emotions. It calms the heart and helps to lower high blood pressure.
- *Sandalwood* is good for sleep and relaxation.
- *Clary sage* promotes feelings of well-being, calms nerves, lifts the mood and diminishes stress.

AROMATHERAPY FOR DEPRESSION

- *Jasmine* is very good for depression because it is uplifting and soothing.
- *Lemon* is uplifting.

- *Bergamont* relaxes the nervous system, is good for anxiety and is uplifting.
- *Neroli* relieves depression, insomnia, stress and anxiety.

AROMATHERAPY FOR MOTIVATION AND ENERGY

- *Ginger* quickens and sharpens the senses. It also helps memory.
- *Rosemary* clears the brain and enhances memory.
- *Peppermint* energizes.

Essential oils are very strong and concentrated, so they should be mixed with a carrier oil such as almond oil (15 drops to 4 ounces of oil). Just add a few drops of the essential oil and massage the body. You may also inhale using a steam inhaler or a diffuser. Only inhale the oil for short periods of time. People with medical conditions such as blood pressure problems or asthma may have reactions to essential oils. Consult your healthcare professional if you have any doubts.

AROMATHERAPY FOR THE WHOLE BODY

Here's another wonderful way to soak away your stress in a special bath. If you are suffering from too little sleep, high stress levels, poor diet, too much caffeine or alcohol, frequent flus or colds, this bath will alkalinize an over-acidic body. You will feel remarkably energized and refreshed. Take this bath periodically to keep your acid alkaline level in balance. Pain and stress cause acidity in the body. This can translate into degenerative disease. This bath can help prevent needless suffering.

Fill the tub with comfortably hot water, enough to cover your reclining body. Pour 10 ounces of baking soda into the water and stir with your hand to dissolve it. Soak for fifteen to twenty minutes for your initial bath. When you step out of the tub, be sure to support yourself because you may be weak or lightheaded from the quick release of the acids or toxins coupled with the heat. Wrap in a big towel and slowly sip an 8-ounce glass of room temperature spring water. Then simply rest for thirty minutes.

FLOWER POWER FOR EMOTIONAL RELIEF

I want to introduce you to a concept that has been known since the 1930s. I am sure you will be intrigued by what you are about to read. I am about to share with you the simple and natural method of establishing equilibrium and harmony by means of wild flowers. That's right, wild flowers—*Bach Flower Essences*.[6]

Not only are they healing to use because of their beauty, but Dr. Edward Bach, a medical doctor and bacteriologist, gave up his lucrative practice to study their emotional link to ill health in the early part of the 1900s. He believed that if a person's emotional balance was corrected, her body's natural, God-given ability to throw off illness would be strengthened.

In the 1930s, Dr. Bach discovered what he called flower essences near the pastoral cottage he maintained in Oxfordshire, England. He truly was a pioneer in the field of mind/body medicine. His findings were very much in tune with the philosophy of natural health. Today, Dr. Bach's gentle essences are used all over the world. The Bach Centre, based in the Oxfordshire cottage where Dr. Bach spent his last years, has received thousands of testimonials from patients and practitioners all vouching for the effectiveness of the Bach Flower Essences. I have used Rescue Remedy, the most popular of all the formulas. God has provided everything we need for the balance of our body, mind and spirit, and I consider these flower essences as one of His many gifts to us for times of emotional distress.

Nevertheless, these essences do not replace the need for prayer when you are in emotional turmoil. With that being said, let's delve deeper.

The Bach Flower Essences consist of thirty-eight essences, including the Rescue Remedy, which I will discuss later. They are homeopathically prepared from the flowers of nonpoisonous plants, bushes and trees. Each is prepared for a specific mental and emotional state. The individual essences relieve the effects that negative emotions or attitudes have on the mind and body. This allows the body's own physical system to fight disease and its associated stress.

Bach Flower Essences are safe, natural, have no side effects and will not interfere with any other nutritional, herbal or prescription medication treatment. What's more, you don't have to be physically ill to benefit from the essences. In times of emotional difficulty, they can help restore balance before any physical symptoms appear.

QUESTIONNAIRE AND GUIDE TO YOUR OWN PERSONAL FORMULA

When you first begin reading the essence descriptions, it may seem as if they all apply to you. However, you should try to limit your combination to a maximum of six or seven essences if you can. Look through the following listing and check the questions that you feel strongly apply to you at this moment. If you answer yes to all questions in any one group, then this essence should be a part of your formula.[7]

AGRIMONY

This formula is for those who hide worries behind a brave face or who are distressed by arguments, quarrels and confrontation. They often turn to alcohol, drugs or comfort eating to help cope.

- ❏ Do you hide your worries behind a cheerful, smiling face to conceal your pain from others?
- ❏ Are you distressed by arguments and quarrels, often giving in to avoid any conflict?
- ❏ When you feel life's pressures weighing you down, do you often turn to drugs, alcohol or other outside influences to help you cope?

ASPEN

These individuals experience apprehension for no known reason. They are seized by sudden fears and anxieties and have feelings of unexplained anxious anticipation, foreboding and dread.

- ❏ Do you have feelings of apprehension, anticipation or uneasiness with no known cause?
- ❏ Do you worry that something bad may happen, but you're not sure what?
- ❏ Do you awaken with a sense of fear and anxiety of what the day will bring?

BEECH

These individuals are critical and intolerant of others, unable and unwilling to make allowances. They are convinced that they are right and everyone else is wrong. They are perfectionists to the extreme.

❑ Are you annoyed by the habits and shortcomings of others?
❑ Do you find yourself being overly critical and intolerant, usually looking for what someone has done wrong and not right?
❑ Do you prefer to work or be alone because the seeming foolishness of others irritates you?

CENTAURY

These people are weak-willed, exploited or imposed upon. Usually timid, quiet and passive, these people act out of subservience rather than a spirit of willing cooperation.

❑ Are you unable to say no to those who constantly impose upon your good nature?
❑ Do you tend to be timid and shy, easily influenced by those stronger in nature than yourself?
❑ Do you often deny your own needs in order to please others?

CERATO

This formula is for those who doubt their own judgment and seek confirmation of others. These people may be wise, educated and intuitive, yet they constantly seek and follow the advice of others rather than trust themselves.

❑ Do you constantly question your own decisions and judgment?
❑ Are you often seeking advice and confirmation from other people, mistrusting your own wisdom?
❑ Do you change direction often, first going one way, then another because you lack the confidence in yourself to stick with one direction?

CHERRY PLUM

These people experience uncontrolled, irrational thoughts. They feel they may explode and give way to violent impulses and fits of rage. NOTE: If symptoms are severe, help from a good therapist is recommended.

❑ Do you fear losing control of yourself?
❑ Are you afraid of hurting yourself or others?
❑ Do you have a tendency to act irrationally and violently, exploding into unexplained fits of rage and anger?

CHESTNUT BUD

These individuals refuse to learn by experience and continually repeat the same mistakes. They do their best to forget past difficulties and thus have no solid basis for future decisions.

❑ Do you find yourself making the same mistakes over and over again, such as choosing the wrong type of partner or staying in a job you dislike?
❑ Do you fail to learn from your experiences?
❑ Does it take you longer to advance in your life because you are slow to learn from past mistakes?

CHICORY

These individuals are overly possessive (self-centered), clinging and overly protective, especially of loved ones. They expect others to conform to their values and are critical and argumentative when they do not. They are interfering, talkative, self-pitying and easily offended.

❑ Are you possessive and manipulative of those you care for?
❑ Do you need to be needed?
❑ Do you feel unloved and unappreciated by your loved ones after all you've done for them?

CLEMATIS

This person is inattentive, dreamy, absent-minded and exercises mental escapism. She likes to be alone and avoids confrontation by withdrawing. You can note her lack of interest.

❑ Do you often feel spacey and out of touch with the real world?
❑ Do you find yourself preoccupied and dreamy, unable to concentrate for any length of time?
❑ Are you drowsy and listless, sleeping more often then necessary?

CRAB APPLE

This person is the cleanser. She experiences self-disgust and self-detestation. She's ashamed of ailments. Her symptoms may include obsessive housecleaning, frequent hand washing or obsession with trivialities.

❑ Are you obsessed with cleanliness?
❑ Are you embarrassed and ashamed of yourself physically, finding yourself unattractive?
❑ Do you tend to concentrate on small physical conditions such as pimples or marks, neglecting more serious problems?

Elm

This one is overwhelmed by responsibility. When people, even those with above average ability, take on too much work while neglecting themselves, the results are often temporary depression, exhaustion and loss of self-esteem.

❑ Are you often overwhelmed by your responsibilities?
❑ Do you feel inadequate when it comes to dealing with the tasks ahead of you?
❑ Do you become depressed and exhausted when faced with your everyday commitments?

Gentian

These people face despondency. They become easily depressed and discouraged when things go wrong or difficulties arise. They are easily disheartened by small setbacks.

❑ Do you become discouraged and depressed when things go wrong?
❑ Are you easily disheartened when faced with difficult situations?
❑ Does your pessimistic attitude prevent you from making an effort to accomplish something?

Gorse

This formula is for those with pessimism, defeatism or "Oh, what's the use?" attitude. Very often these are people suffering from a chronic illness and have been told (or have come to believe) that nothing can be done for them. They have no faith that the treatments they are undergoing will work.

❑ Do you feel despondent and hopeless, at the end of your rope both mentally and physically?
❑ Do you lack confidence that things will get better in your life and therefore make no effort to improve your circumstances?

❑ Do you believe that nothing can be done to relieve your pain and suffering?

HEATHER

This person is talkative and obsessed with her own troubles and experiences. She needs an audience and dislikes being alone, but she fails to realize she is often avoided because she saps other people's vitality.

❑ Are you totally self-absorbed, concerned only about yourself and your own problems and ailments?
❑ Do you talk incessantly and are not interested in what anyone else has to say?
❑ Do you dislike being alone and are always seeking the companionship of others?

HOLLY

Unconsciously, these people suffer from insecurity, yet project aggression to the world at large. They lack the ability to feel love.

❑ Are you full of jealousy and hate?
❑ Do you mistrust others' intentions, feeling that people have ulterior motives?
❑ Do you feel enormous anger toward other people?

HONEYSUCKLE

These individuals are living in the past—nostalgic, homesick. They lack the ability to change the present because they are constantly looking at the past, usually out of a sense of fear.

❑ Do you find yourself living in the past, nostalgic and homesick for the way it was?
❑ Are you unable to change present circumstances because you are always looking back and never forward?
❑ Are you dissatisfied with your accomplishments?

HORNBEAM

These people have a Monday-morning feeling, and their dominant emotion is procrastination. They find it difficult to face everyday problems and responsibilities, but they do manage to get things done.

❑ Do you often feel too tired to face the day ahead?
❑ Do you feel overworked or bored with your life?
❑ Do you lack enthusiasm and therefore tend to procrastinate?

IMPATIENS

Impatient, irritable, capable and efficient, these people act, think and speak quickly but are frustrated and irritated by slow coworkers. They often wind up working alone.

❑ Are you impatient and irritable with others who seem to do things too slowly for you?
❑ Do you prefer to work alone?
❑ Do you feel a sense of urgency in everything you do, always rushing to get through things?

LARCH

These people share a lack of self-confidence and feel inferior. They fear failure. They may be secretly aware that they really do have the ability they admire (without envy) in others, but these people simply won't try for fear of failing.

❑ Do you lack self-confidence?
❑ Do you feel inferior and often become discouraged?
❑ Are you so sure that you will fail and therefore do not even attempt things?

MIMILUS

These people fear known things. They are marked by shyness and timidity. They fear accidents, pain, poverty, public speaking and unemployment. They are often artistic and talented, but can be tongue-tied and unable to speak about their fears.

❑ Do you have fears of known things such as illness, death, pain, heights, darkness and the dentist?
❑ Are you shy, overly sensitive and often afraid?
❑ When you are confronted with a frightening situation, do you become too paralyzed to act?

MUSTARD

These individuals feel a dark cloud that descends, making them sad and low for no known reason. Although this depression can often lift just as suddenly as it descends, people who suffer from it are truly exposed to the deepest gloom.

❑ Do you feel deep gloom that seems to quickly descend for no apparent reason and lifts just as suddenly?
❑ Do you feel your moods swinging back and forth?
❑ Do you feel depressed without knowing why?

Oak

Normally strong and courageous, these people feel they are no longer able to struggle bravely against illness and/or adversity. They are overachievers with a strong sense of duty. They hide their fatigue because they are afraid to appear weak to others.

❑ Are you exhausted but feel the need to struggle on against all odds?
❑ Do you have a strong sense of duty and dependability, carrying on no matter what obstacles stand in your way?
❑ Do you neglect your own needs in order to complete a task?

Olive

This person feels fatigued and drained of energy. This exhaustion sets in after a prolonged period of strain. Everything feels like a monumental effort. Life lacks zest.

❑ Do you feel utterly and completely exhausted?
❑ Are you totally drained of all energy with no reserves left, finding it difficult to carry on?
❑ Is everything an effort? Does your life lack zest?

Pine

This individual has a guilt complex and blames herself even for the mistakes of others. She is always apologizing. These people feel undeserving and unworthy, which in turn destroys the joy of living.

❑ Are you full of guilt and self-reproach?
❑ Do you blame yourself for everything that goes wrong, including the mistakes of others?
❑ Do you set overly high standards for yourself and are never satisfied with your achievements?

Red Chestnut

These people constantly fear the worst, living in dreaded anticipation of some nonspecific but definitely unfortunate thing happening to their loved ones.

❏ Are you excessively concerned and worried for your loved ones?
❏ Do you constantly worry that harm may come to those you care for?
❏ Are you distressed and disturbed by other people's problems?

Rock rose

The primary emotions are sudden alarm, fright and panic. Often these feelings occur after being in an accident or narrowly avoiding or witnessing an accident. This person feels an acute threat, sickness or natural disaster, and these emotions can cause him to feel frozen and helpless with fear.

❏ Do you feel terror and panic?
❏ Do you become helpless and frozen in the face of your fear?
❏ Do you suffer from nightmares?

Rock water

These people are self-dominating to the point of self-martyrdom. Opinionated and dogmatic, they are much too self-concerned to connect with other people's lives.

❏ Are you inflexible in your approach to life, always striving for perfection?
❏ Are you so rigid in your ideals that you deny yourself the simple pleasures of life?
❏ Are you overly concerned with diet, exercise, work and spiritual disciplines?

Scleranthus

Primary emotions include uncertainty, indecision and vacillation. These folks experience many fluctuating moods and often waste time and miss opportunities because their up-and-down mood swings make them unreliable.

❏ Do you find it difficult to decide when faced with a choice of two possibilities?

❏ Do you lack concentration, always fidgety and nervous?
❏ Do your moods change from one extreme to another, from joy to sadness, optimism to pessimism or laughing to crying?

STAR OF BETHLEHEM

This formula is for all the effects of serious news or fright following an accident. There are those who suffer serious distress and unhappiness under adverse conditions.

❏ Have you suffered a shock in your life such as an accident, loss of a loved one, terrible news or illness?
❏ Are you numbed or withdrawn as a result of recent traumatic events in your life?
❏ Have you suffered a loss or grief that you have never recovered from?

SWEET CHESTNUT

Primary emotions include utter dejection and a bleak outlook. Anguish is so great that it seems unbearable; all endurance seems gone.

❏ Do you suffer from extreme mental anguish?
❏ Do you feel that you have reached the limits of what you could possibly endure?
❏ Do you feel as though the future holds nothing for you?

VERVAIN

This formula addresses over-enthusiasm and fanatical beliefs. These are strong-willed people with strong views, especially about what they consider to be injustice. They are often so enthusiastic that they alienate potential allies.

❏ Do you feel tense and highly strung?
❏ Do you have strong opinions, and only yours are the right ones?
❏ Is your over-enthusiasm almost to the point of being fanatical?

VINE

These individuals are dominating, inflexible, tyrannical, autocratic and arrogant. They are capable, gifted and ambitious people who use their abilities to bully others. In addition, they are proud and usually ruthlessly greedy for power.

❑ Do you tend to be domineering and overbearing?
❑ Do you feel the need to always be right?
❑ Are you inflexible and feel you know more than anyone else?

Walnut

This formula assists in adjustment to transition or change, such as puberty, menopause, divorce or new surroundings. It's also for those with definite ideas but who are occasionally diverted by the strong opinions of others.

❑ Are you experiencing any change in your life such as a move, new job, loss of a loved one, new relationship—divorce, puberty, menopause or giving up an addiction?
❑ Are you distracted by outside influences?
❑ Do you need to make a break from strong forces or attachments in your life that may be holding you back?

Water violet

This person is proud, reserved and enjoys being alone. Often gentle and self-reliant, she nevertheless can exude a sense of superiority that makes her appear aloof and condescending.

❑ Do you appear to others to be aloof and overly proud?
❑ Do you have a tendency to be withdrawn and prefer to be alone when faced with too many external distractions?
❑ Do you bear your grief and sorrow in silence?

White chestnut

This formula is for those with persistent unwanted thoughts or preoccupation with some worry or episode. This person conducts mental arguments that go around and around and lead to a troubled, depressed mind.

❑ Do you find your head full of persistent, unwanted thoughts that prevent concentration?
❑ Do you relive unhappy events or arguments over and over again?
❑ Are you unable to sleep at times because your mind seems to be cluttered with mental arguments that go round and round?

Wild oat

This formula helps one determine one's intended path in life. There are people who have ambition and talents, but who waste those gifts through a lack of direction. They are frustrated because they are aware that life is passing them by.

❑ Do you find yourself in a complete state of uncertainty over major life decisions?
❑ Are you displeased with your lifestyle and feel dissatisfied with your achievements?
❑ Do you have ambition but feel that life is passing you by?

WILD ROSE

These primary emotions are resignation and apathy. Whether it's illness, a monotonous life or poor working conditions, these people do not complain but simply plod unhappily on. Their apathetic behavior assures that their condition will not change. They will miss even the simplest of life's pleasures.

❑ Are you apathetic and resigned to whatever may happen in your life?
❑ Do you have the attitude, "I will just live with it"?
❑ Do you lack the motivation to improve the quality of your life?

WILLOW

These folks feel resentment, bitterness and a "poor old me attitude!" They can start to begrudge other people's good fortune. Grumbling and irritable, they enjoy spreading gloom.

❑ Do you feel resentful and bitter?
❑ Do you have difficulty forgiving and forgetting?
❑ Do you feel life is unfair and find yourself taking less and less interest in the things you used to enjoy?

RESCUE REMEDY

This formula is for people who find themselves in emergency stress situations. It is the only Bach essences combination. It includes these essences: cherry plum, clematis, impatiens, rock rose and star of Bethlehem. It was formulated and recognized by Dr. Bach himself. Rescue Remedy will comfort, reassure and calm those who have received serious news, severe upset, startling experiences and have consequently fallen into a numbed, bemused state of mind. Rescue Remedy can also be used just before bed to calm a troubled mind or before any stressful situation such as exams, doctor or dentist appointments or public speaking. Rescue Remedy also comes in cream form that can be used topically on burns, stings, sprains or even as a massage cream.

HOW TO TAKE THE BACH FLOWER ESSENCES

The essences can be prepared two ways. Add two drops of the chosen essences to a glass of water or juice and sip throughout the day. You can also place two drops of each essence into a 1-ounce amber glass-dropper bottle filled three-quarters full with spring water. You can combine six to seven essences in your dosage bottle. (If you choose Rescue Remedy as part of your formula, it would be considered one essence and you would use four drops). You may want to add a teaspoon of brandy, apple cider vinegar or vegetable glycerin as a preservative. This is your treatment bottle. This should be taken by mouth a minimum of four times per day, four drops each time, particularly upon rising in the morning and before bedtime.

For those unable to swallow or who are alcohol sensitive, the essences can be applied externally by moistening the lips, wrists and temples.

Now let's review your protocol for dangerous emotions.

CHAPTER 6

Your Personal Protocol to Replenish Your Brain

In this chapter we will take a look at the most important things we have learned about brain health so that you can develop your personal plan for better health.

GABA

Since the amino acid GABA affects our mind, memory, mood and behavior, and because stress, trauma and anxiety deplete our supply of GABA, I recommend that you supplement with GABA in this very first stage. GABA has a natural, calming effect, and it helps to cool the brain. Remember that amino acid deficiencies occur when we experience long periods of pain, stress, depression or anxiety. Once depletion occurs, the brain is then overwhelmed by anxiety signals, leaving you tense and out of control.

Your brain needs more than 100 milligrams of GABA to restore it to the proper level. I recommend capsules over tablets for easier assimilation. This is true for all of my supplement recommendations.

LIQUID SEROTONIN

If you are not currently on SSRI medication, commonly known as selective serotonin reuptake inhibitors, you may take liquid serotonin. Serotonin is a key neurotransmitter in brain function that enhances focus, elevates mood and reduces anger and aggression. It can also help reduce cravings for carbohydrates and alcohol.

MAGNESIUM GEL CAPS

Take 400 milligrams at bedtime. Low magnesium levels are found in persons with hyperirritability, depression and anxiety. In addition, magnesium helps the muscles to relax.

BRAIN LINK

This is a total amino acid complex that blankets your system with all of the amino acids that create neurotransmitter links for enhanced brain function. Used daily, it is a total formula that can be used along with the abovementioned supplements.

ANXIETY CONTROL 24

This is an amino acid support formula that contains amino acids, herbs, vitamins and minerals along with essential cofactors to help relax the anxious mind or stressed body. Billie J. Sahley formulated the formula. It contains the herbs passionflower and *primula officinalis,* which support an overstressed body and calm the central nervous systems naturally. It is a formula that can be used day or night to fill the deficiencies caused by our stressful lives. It is also wonderful for anxious or active teens. I only wish I had this formula during my teen years!

VITAMIN B$_6$

This must be taken with amino acids. You may take a B-complex formula that contains vitamin B$_6$ and the full spectrum of B vitamins.

MASSAGE

Consider having a weekly massage. It will help your muscles relax, thereby relieving tension.

EXERCISE

Exercise is one of the best stress relievers in the world. The more you exercise, the more energy you will have.

EATING PLAN

Follow my eating plan as outlined.

MANTLE TECHNIQUE

Tense and hold for the count of ten each muscle group individually.

STRESS-RELIEVING BATH

This should be used periodically to keep your acid/alkaline level in balance.

PRAYER

Always stay in prayer.

ADRENAL HEALTH

Take pantothenic acid, B complex, vitamin C, Royal Jelly and astragalus. Add dietary recommendations listed in the adrenal section. Choose the essential oil that suits your current situation and use as directed.

HORMONAL HELP

I recommend that you use Dr. Janet's Balanced by Nature Progesterone Cream.

BACH ESSENCES

Choose the ones that suit your current situation.

CONCLUSION

Now that you've learned how to replenish a depleted brain, read on to discover the importance of renewing your mind.

PART TWO
RETHINK AND RENEW

CHAPTER 7

As a Man Thinketh

This section will focus on changing your thought patterns, also known as renewing the mind. You must consciously choose forgiveness and love over the dangerous emotions that ultimately destroy your health and your life. Research shows us:

- Minnesota's St. Olaf College found that people who shared tales with others felt happier and less stressed. A separate study by the same experts revealed that those who merely listened to heart-warming stories experienced a drop in both blood pressure and heart rate. In other words, your mind and body say, *Thanks for the memories.*

- Researchers from the University of Michigan found that donating your time and energy to worthy causes feels good and just might add years to your life. In the study of more than one thousand people aged sixty-five and older, those who volunteered up to forty hours a year were less likely to die during the following seven and a half years than people who didn't volunteer at all!

- According to research out of the University of North Dakota, patients with asthma or rheumatoid arthritis who wrote about traumatic moments had great health gains compared to those who made notes on neutral topics. In other words, putting stress-provoking thoughts on paper may help heal what ails you.[1]

In James Allen's classic book *As a Man Thinketh,* he states:

> Disease and health are rooted in thought. Sickly thoughts will express themselves through a sickly body. Thoughts of fear have been known to kill a man as speedily as a bullet, and they are continually killing thousands of people as surely though less rapidly. The people who live in fear of disease are the people who get it. Anxiety quickly demoralizes the whole body and lays it open to the entrance of disease; while impure thoughts, even if not physically indulged, will soon affect the nervous system.[2]

YOUR THOUGHTS ARE KEY

Thoughts of love cause your body to release interleuken and interferon. These are healing substances to the body. Anxious thoughts cause your body to release cortisone and adrenaline, which suppress your immune response. Peaceful, tranquil thoughts release chemicals in your body similar to Valium, which helps your body relax and adjust.

In Dean Ornish's book *Love & Survival: 8 Pathways to Intimacy and Health,* he says that love is the missing piece in our frazzled, busy world.[3] Dr. Ornish is most commonly known and associated with the famous low-fat diet. But Ornish has always suspected that more than diet was responsible for his patients' recoveries. He believes that the most powerful results occur when his patients open their hearts emotionally.

He states, "I am not aware of any other factor in medicine—not diet, not smoking, not exercise, not stress, not genetics, not drugs, not surgery—that has a greater impact on our quality of life, incidence of illness and premature death from all causes." He goes on to say that in study after study, people who feel lonely or isolated are three to five times more likely to get sick and die prematurely, not only from heart disease but from virtually all causes, when compared to those who have a sense of love, connection and community. He believes there is nothing in medicine that has that powerful an effect.

Bringing love and intimacy into our lives is a challenge. People have become very adept at isolating themselves from other people by not allowing them to get too close. But, when we wall ourselves off emotionally to protect ourselves we may be actually threatening our survival. Ornish feels that if we understand that the consequences of not opening up are much more dire than those of opening up, then that may motivate us to have the courage to open up to our loved ones and to make this a priority in our lives.

Dr. Ornish believes, as do I, that our childhood experiences define our capacity for intimacy as adults. In Ornish's book he helps us understand how early life experiences get in the way of intimacy as adults. Ornish developed these eight pathways to intimacy after transforming himself at his core. I have listed these pathways for you. For additional help, you may find Dr. Ornish's books at any major bookstore across the country.

- *Communicate with compassion.* Tell another person what you are really feeling and show respect for their feelings by listening carefully to what they say to you.
- *Get together*. A support group can help you to overcome isolation. When people open their hearts to each other, intimacy follows.
- *Confess and forgive.* When you share your secrets and mistakes with another person, you form a powerful and intimate bond.
- *Serve.* When you help others you help yourself. Serving others is one of the sweet ways to overcome loneliness and isolation.
- *Get therapy.* Unresolved issues make intimacy difficult. An unloving family, low self-esteem and grief can be addressed by a skilled psychotherapist.

- *Touch.* Lack of caring physical contact with another person can lead to isolation, illness and even death.
- *Make a commitment.* Until you commit to someone, you are not vulnerable. Until you are vulnerable, you can't have intimacy.
- *Meditate or pray.* Prayer or meditation helps you to feel connected.[4]

When it comes to your health, your thoughts are key. The Bible tells us to fix our thoughts on what is true and honorable and right. Think about things that are pure and lovely and admirable. Think about things that are excellent and worthy of praise. (See Philippians 4:8.)

You must consciously monitor your thoughts on a daily basis. When you are first regaining your emotional health, it may take minute-to-minute monitoring until you get control. One way to overcome playing old tapes of pain, self-doubt and anxiety is to go deep into the Word of God. Invest in inspirational tapes or praise and worship music. Listen to testimonies of how God heals today as He did in the past. He is the same yesterday, today and forever. So, it follows that we can be healed of our past, be set free in the present and be all that we can be in the future. In other words, whole, healed and free!

As we work on spiritual and emotional health, the body must be addressed also. You have to use a three-pronged body, mind and spirit approach. You can get better. Because you have been through the fire of trauma and emotional pain, you will be a better, stronger and more compassionate person.

CHOOSE LOVE

> Many waters cannot quench love; rivers cannot wash it away.
>
> —Song of Solomon 8:7

There is a great difference between running scared and being informed. There is a sense of relief and freedom that comes

104

from being armed with the knowledge that your current state of physical health is a reflection of your emotional health. Once you realize this very important connection, you can take an active part in your healing program.

All of those nasty chronic complaints—headaches, backaches, fatigue, muscle tension, panic attacks, anxiety and depression—are triggered by stress, buried or repressed pain, unforgiveness and grief that was never released and let go. What you won't let go won't let go of you! My message throughout the book is to let go once and for all. Letting go of dangerous emotions will make room for positive emotions to emerge and healing to take place.

Life is always moving forward; it does not stop and look back. It moves forward at a steady pace, and in doing so, it gives us new opportunities to put into use what was learned from past mistakes. Every day is a new beginning, another chance to live in forgiveness, unconditional love and truth. You must learn to love yourself unconditionally, forgive yourself and go forth in truth. In other words, be true to yourself. Never again let anyone or any situation anger you or hurt you to the point that your body, mind and spirit become depleted.

You know now that depletion is a total body experience. No situation is worth draining the very life out of you. Remember that you are learning to love others and even yourself. You wouldn't drain the life out of anyone you love, would you? Love your neighbor as yourself—unconditionally—and your life will change dramatically.

> Love is patient, love is kind, and is not jealous; love does not brag and is not arrogant, does not act unbecomingly; it does not seek its own, is not provoked, does not take into account a wrong suffered, does not rejoice in unrighteousness, but rejoices with the truth; bears all things, believes all things, hopes all things, endures all things. Love never fails.
>
> —1 CORINTHIANS 13:4–8, NAS

The power of love can heal us of the dangerous emotions that threaten to destroy our lives and our health. It is your choice. I recommend that you choose love and live life to the fullest.

LOVE AND THE PURSUIT OF HAPPINESS

When you let go of dangerous emotions, you are then free to experience pure love. It will also be possible to receive love and give love without fear. You will experience a peaceful trust that will replace the mistrust that has held you captive in the past. You will feel more relaxed and at peace in your relationships with your friends, family and loved ones. Once you are free to accept and to give love, you will begin to allow this love to flow out of you and into the lives of everyone and everything you come into contact with.

This is actually the way God made us to be. We thrive mentally, physically and spiritually when we develop a lifestyle of loving people unconditionally. Everyone desires love and needs to be loved. You will be amazed at the transformation that takes place in your life. People will be drawn to you. Love is the universal language. It is a healing balm.

In his book *A Journey to the Other Side of Life,* Kevin Lane Turner states:

> You may fear that this activity will draw other people to you in an unhealthy fashion. You may fear that an unhealthy emotional dependence is developing. This is not true. Unhealthy emotional dependencies develop when two people are both emotionally unhealthy, unbalanced, and wounded. One who is genuinely whole, healed and free and at peace will not allow this activity to occur by instinct and decision, the healed individual wants to draw the wounded individual into wholeness, healing, freedom, peace, and love, not into an unhealthy dependence…This can only occur as the wounded individual links up emotionally with his or her Creator and experiences genuine and permanent healing, freedom, peace, and love emotionally. The healed person knows this and abides by this.[5]

We can only be truly healed emotionally once the core or root issue has been resolved or dealt with. Only then can true love and happiness be experienced, not some pseudo-happiness that we wear like a mask for others. Such masks are barricades or walls that hinder love from being given or received. You have heard that it is better to give than to receive. This is especially true when it comes to love because giving love produces healing and change. This is because love is unconditional giving. Love is the healing emotion that literally cancels out dangerous ones. It is so powerful that it controls and eliminates fear.

Can you truly be healed? I believe that you can, but you must have the willingness and desire to do so. You must do the work. No, it is not easy. It may be the most difficult task you have undertaken. Looking deep within yourself takes a lot of courage. That is where God comes in and holds you up as you go deep within. With God's help, the process is accelerated. So, prayer and a close walk with God are imperative. You will then experience life as God intended it to be, for you will be all that He created you to be.

DANGEROUS EMOTIONS AND THE ILLNESS CONNECTION

Dangerous emotions can create a pathway to illness. Let's investigate.

HOW DO YOU BECOME ILL?

- Blame other people for your problems.
- Do not express your feelings and views openly and honestly.
- Be resentful and hypercritical, especially toward yourself.
- If you are overstressed and tired, ignore it and keep pushing yourself.
- Avoid deep, lasting, intimate relationships.
- Worry most, if not all, of the time.
- Follow everyone else's opinion and advice while seeing yourself as miserable and stuck.

- Don't have a sense of humor; life is no laughing matter.
- Do not make any life-enriching changes.

How to become sicker (if you are already sick)

- Dwell upon negative, fearful images.
- Be self-pitying, envious and angry. Blame everyone and everything for your illness.
- Give up all activities that bring you a sense of purpose and fun.
- Cut yourself off from other people.
- Complain about your symptoms.
- Don't take care of yourself because, *What's the use?*
- Listen to conflicting medical opinions and never follow through with any advice.
- See your life as pointless.

How to stay well or get better

- Release all negative emotions, resentment, envy, fear, sadness and anger. Express your feelings; don't hold on to them.
- Do things that bring a sense of fulfillment, joy and purpose and that validate your worth.
- Pay close and loving attention to yourself by nourishing and encouraging yourself.
- Love yourself and love everyone else. Make loving a primary expression in your life.
- Pray and give thanks to God continually.
- Keep a sense of humor.
- Accept yourself and everything in your life as an opportunity for growth and learning.
- Be grateful.
- Make a positive contribution to your community through some sort of work or service that you enjoy.
- Try to heal any wounds from past relationships.[6]

SPIRITUAL FOOD

A famous Chinese professor and herbalist, Li Chung Yun, was reported to have lived to be 256 years old. He attributed his long life to inward calm. In his book titled *Every Woman's Book,* author Paavo Airola had found that all people in all parts of the world who lived extraordinarily long lives had several lifestyle factors in common. They include unadulterated foods, poison-free environment, plenty of exercise, systematic undereating and, most importantly, inward calm. These people were happy with whatever their lot in life was. They did not envy or covet, were respected by friends and family and held important positions in the community.[7]

The whole secret of prolonging one's life is to do nothing to shorten it. I tell my clients to apply this philosophy to their mental, physical and spiritual selves and they have a winning combination!

FOOD FOR THE SOUL

Many times when you are suffering anxiety, depression, stress and resultant physical illness, a spiritual depletion has taken place. We are body, mind and spirit. Neglecting the spiritual portion of your being will not bring wellness. There will always be an emptiness that only God can fill. There is a longing in all of us to be fed spiritually. Many of us are wandering this earth in a state of spiritual depletion. It is an unnatural state of being. No wonder there is an epidemic of depression, anxiety and chronic disease. One-third of our total being is not being fed. The following pages will offer spiritual food to help feed the depletion that accompanies health-destroying emotions.

Research has uncovered one of the greatest healing miracles of all time—spirituality. More than three hundred studies confirm that people of faith are healthier than nonbelievers and less likely to die prematurely from any cause. Having faith can also speed recovery from physical and mental illness, surgery and addiction.

According to Dale A. Matthews, MD, an associate professor of medicine at Georgetown University School of Medicine in Washington DC and author of *The Faith Factor: Proof of the*

Healing Power of Prayer (Viking Penguin, 1998), the body responds positively to faith. Blood pressure and pulse rate tend to be lower, oxygen consumption better, brain wave patterns slower and immune function enhanced if you practice your faith regularly.

Faith also gives you a sense of peace and an ability to help you look beyond your present problems with hope, which can reduce stress and lower your risk of anxiety and depression.

Religiously committed people are less likely to drink and smoke, and they are more likely to take their medicine and wear seat belts than nonreligious people. For many people the church is a place where they feel connected and have a sense of meaning and purpose. They are surrounded by people who care and take an interest in their lives.

WHAT DOES THE BIBLE SAY ABOUT DANGEROUS EMOTIONS?

ANGER

For His anger is but for a moment,
His favor is for life.
Weeping may endure for a night,
But joy comes in the morning.

—PSALM 30:5, NKJV

A fool vents all his feelings,
But a wise man holds them back.

—PROVERBS 29:11, NKJV

He who is often rebuked, and hardens his neck,
Will suddenly be destroyed, and that without remedy.

—PROVERBS 29:1, NKJV

So then, my beloved brethren, let every man be swift to hear, slow to speak, slow to wrath.

—JAMES 1:19, NKJV

Do not let the sun go down on your anger; otherwise, your anger will go deep down inside you.

ANXIETY

> Do not be anxious about anything, but in everything, by prayer and petition, with thanksgiving, present your requests to God. And the peace of God, which transcends all understanding, will guard your hearts and your minds in Christ Jesus.
>
> —PHILIPPIANS 4:6–7

> An anxious heart weighs a man down, but a kind word cheers him up.
>
> —PROVERBS 12:25

> Cast all your anxiety on him because he cares for you.
>
> —1 PETER 5:7

Most of the things we worry about never even happen. For the things that do, God is always there to help you through.

BITTERNESS

> Pursue peace with all people, and holiness, without which no one will see the Lord: looking carefully lest anyone fall short of grace of God; lest any root of bitterness springing up cause trouble, and by this many become defiled.
>
> —HEBREWS 12:14–15, NKJV

Bitterness can destroy us from the inside out. It is like rust that corrodes our spirit, takes away our peace and makes it impossible to have a healthy relationship with anyone. You must not harbor past hurts. That only invites resentment. Instead, use past hurts as opportunities to develop spiritually.

EMOTIONAL BAGGAGE

Emotional baggage consists of feelings, thought patterns and past experiences that continue to traumatize a person each time they are triggered or recalled.

Cast your cares on the LORD and he will sustain you; he will never permit the righteous fall.

—PSALM 55:22

You must deal with your emotional baggage because it will keep you from experiencing a life of freedom.

Are you burned out? Mentally? Physically? Spiritually?

Come to me, all you who are weary and burdened, and I will give you rest.

—MATTHEW 11:28

Make a conscious effort to slow down. Take a step back from everything. You may need to rethink your priorities. You alone are responsible for your burnout.

FEAR

Even though I walk
 through the valley of the shadow of death,
I will fear no evil,
 for you are with me;
your rod and your staff,
 they comfort me.

—PSALM 23:4

The LORD is my light and my salvation—
 whom shall I fear?
The LORD is the stronghold of my life—
 of whom shall I be afraid?

—PSALM 27:1

The fear of the LORD is the beginning of wisdom.

—PSALM 111:10

So do not fear, for I am with you.

—ISAIAH 41:10

Are not five sparrows sold for two pennies? Yet not one of them is forgotten by God. Indeed, the very hairs of your head are all numbered. Don't be afraid; you are worth more than many sparrows.

—Luke 12:6–7

For God hath not given us the spirit of fear; but of power, and of love, and of a sound mind.

—2 Timothy 1:7, KJV

There is no fear in love; but perfect love casts out fear, because fear involves torment. But he who fears has not been made perfect in love.

—1 John 4:18, NKJV

Reject every fear that comes into your mind and tries to take you captive. Rebuke it and ask for the peace of God to surround you.

FRUSTRATION

Be at rest once more, O my soul.

—Psalm 116:7

Oftentimes frustration is a result of our own failures. It is a feeling of irritability and restlessness. Sometimes frustration is a sign that you need to shift gears or that you are not walking on the correct path. In this case, frustration can be a catalyst for change. Restlessness is a challenge for you to change.

GRIEF

In my distress, I called to the LORD, and he answered me. From the depths of the grave I called for help, and you listened to my cry.

—Jonah 2:2

Grief is a fact of life. Although it is never a pleasant experience, it is a process that you must allow yourself to walk through. If you do not allow yourself time to grieve, you will carry it with you only to have it resurface over and over. This will only prolong your grief. So, grieve for a season. It is only natural. Then as days pass you will know when it is time to move forward again.

GUILT

> I, even I, am he who blots out
> your transgressions, for my own sake,
> and remembers your sins no more.
> —ISAIAH 43:25

You must forgive yourself because if you have repented of your sins, God has forgiven and forgotten them. So why haven't you?

LONELINESS

> He Himself has said, "I will never leave you nor forsake you."
> —HEBREWS 13:5, NKJV

Loneliness can open the door to all kinds of maladies in your body, mind and spirit. It has been linked to the most dreaded disease of our day—cancer. Take comfort that even when it seems that everyone has abandoned you, it is impossible to be alone once you ask God to come into your life and live in you. This is the most intimate relationship in all the world. No one or no thing will even begin to compare to this most intimate of relationships.

UNFORGIVENNESS

> Forgive us our debts, as we also have forgiven our debtors.
> —MATTHEW 6:12

> For if you forgive men when they sin against you, your heavenly Father will also forgive you. But if you do not forgive men their sins, your Father will not forgive your sins.
> —MATTHEW 6:14

> Then Peter came to Jesus and asked, "Lord, how many times shall I forgive my brother when he sins against me? Up to seven times?" Jesus answered, "I tell you, not seven times, but seventy-seven times."
> —MATTHEW 18:21–22

I cannot stress this point enough—unforgiveness will destroy your mind, body and spirit. More importantly, if you do not forgive, you will not be forgiven. If God forgives, why can't you?

Forgiveness is a primary key to overcoming dangerous emotions. Forgiveness is not only good for your mind, it also is good for your body and soul. Sometimes it isn't easy, but there is good reason to forgive one another. A new study out of the University of Tennessee tracked subjects' blood pressure and heart rate as they discussed being betrayed by a parent, friend or lover. As the interviews began, blood pressure shot up for all of the participants. But the levels for those who forgave soon returned to normal. The readings for subjects who were grudge holders stayed high. Interestingly enough, women were more likely to be unforgiving than men. By this one study, you can see how resentment and unforgiveness can take a physical toll.[8]

CHAPTER 8

Ban Cluttered Thinking

In today's world, the overwhelming amount of information we encounter can be another source of stress, and long-term stress can be a key factor in many diseases from heart disease to cancer. Take steps now to ban the cluttered thought processes in your mind that lead to stress and breakdown. Use the following suggestions to start.

1. *Prepare.* Take five minutes at the end of each day to prepare for the next. Determine what has priority and make a short list of things to accomplish the next day. Do not make a long overwhelming list. This will only worsen the situation you are trying to rectify.

2. *Balance the scale.* Make a list of your priorities in your life so you can see them. What does your list show? Are you working most of the time and not taking time for family fun? This balancing exercise will help you see just how out of balance your priorities have become. With the knowledge comes the realization that you must make changes to safeguard not only your health but your family relationships as well.

3. *Early to bed; early to rise.* Go to bed a little earlier and practice my MANTLE technique, commonly known as progressive muscle relaxation, while lying in bed. Wake up earlier and use the technique again to keep your body stretched and tension free.

4. *Take a vacation with God.* Take just ten minutes every few hours during the day to go on vacation with God. Pray or meditate on His Word or simply quiet your mind and enjoy being in His presence. I promise you, a refreshing will take place.

TAKE A MENTAL TIMEOUT

Webster defines *stress* as "that which strains or deforms." Too much stress on a piece of metal causes it to break. Place too much stress on your body or mind, and it begins to suffer consequences such as fatigue, tension and anxiety and illness. Many times the worst source of stress is in our own minds.

Do you find your thoughts leaping from one subject to the next? While you may sometimes dwell on happy thoughts, often the ones that trap you are the distressing ones. It's almost as if the mind is behaving like a yo-yo, taking you from the highest of heights to the depths of despair all in a twenty-four-hour period.

The "should-have, could-have" thoughts that keep us in anguish over our pasts, which we seem to have no power to change, are the most destructive ones. They cause us to waste precious time and energy that could be used to build healthy new relationships that would help us to live more healthy, satisfying lives.

When you find your thoughts bouncing up an down like a yo-yo, simply stop and take a mental timeout known as taking a little mini-meditation break several times during the day. It's like taking a breath of fresh mental air, according to Jon Kabat-Zinn, PhD, director of the Stress Reduction Clinic at the University of Massachusetts Medical Center and author of *Full Catastrophe Living* (Delta Books).

Here are a few recommended suggestions to help to ease you into the routine of practicing mini-meditations throughout your day.

- *Learn to live in the moment.*
- *Look and listen.* Watch clouds, flames of a fire or waves breaking on the shore. Just let yourself get lost in the experience as you did in childhood.
- *Food for thought.* When you take a bite of your favorite ripe fruit or spoonful of your favorite dessert, don't just gulp it down barely even noticing the taste and texture. Focus your attention on the sweet aroma and taste as if you were tasting it for the very first time.
- *Wash dishes and relax.* Focus on the way that you do dishes. Feel the warm soapy water. Notice the weight and appearance of the different objects as you wash them. Stay focused and relaxed. Live in the moment. When you're finished, watch the water and soap go down the drain and envision your problems and worries following close behind.
- *Pay attention to Mother Nature.* Pay close attention to trees, leaves, grass, ponds and lakes. Watch birds fly and butterflies flutter from flower to flower.
- *Watch a loved one breathe.* Lie beside your child, relative, husband or wife and simply watch their chest as they breathe. Get close enough to hear each breath. Breath is life. This is a very grounding experience!

LIVING IN THE MOMENT

A wonderful example of living life in the moment found its way to me while I was writing this book. The author was Nadine Stair, an eighty-five-year-old woman who penned this poem while confronting her death. There is so much to learn from this wise woman.

> If I had my life to live over, I'd try to make more mistakes
> next time.

I would relax, I would limber up and I would be crazier than
    I have been on this trip.
I know very few things I'd take seriously anymore.
I would take more chances, I would take more trips, I would
    scale more mountains, I would swim more rivers and I
    would watch more sunsets.
I would eat more ice cream and fewer beans.
I would have more actual troubles and fewer imaginary
    ones.

You see, I was one of those people who lived prophylactically,
    sensibly and sanely hour after hour and day after day.
Oh, I've had my moments, and if I had it to do all over again
    I'd have many more of them.
In fact, I'd try not to have anything else just moments, one
    after another, instead of living so many years ahead of
    my day.
I've been one of those people who never went anywhere
    without a thermometer, a hot water bottle, a gargle, a
    raincoat and a parachute.
If I had it to do all over again, I'd travel lighter, much lighter,
    than I have.
I would start barefoot earlier in the spring, and I'd stay that
    way later in the fall.
And, I would ride more merry-go-rounds and catch more
    gold rings and greet more people and pick more
    flowers and dance more often.

If I had it to do all over again.
But you see—I don't.

Nadine's words are thought-provoking.

WHAT WE FEED, WE GROW

You must learn to change channels when your past hurt, anger,
unforgiveness, trauma and grief resurface. Choose to forgive, and
then let it go. You must not dwell on the past. Do not relive it.

Change the channel in your mind to forgiveness, or bitterness will set in. Remember, what you won't let go of won't let go of you.

Jesus said that we should forgive seventy times seven and that we will be shown the same amount of mercy that we have shown others.

You have the ability to forgive and let go. Again, it is a conscious choice. But do you have the desire? Life is too short. If you live a life of unconditional love, you will reap a life of freedom and abundance.

See the best in people. Repay evil with goodness and mercy. It is a small price to pay when you consider the reward of sound emotional health and a body that is free of disease.

In a magazine article titled "Can I get my dad back?," Deepak Chopra, MD, states, "If you really want to healed, you will have to take total responsibility for whatever you experience. These are your feelings. You have to deal with them. Blaming someone else for what's happening inside you will never allow you to go beyond the hurt."[1]

He also says that you need to articulate your emotions, preferably in written form. He recommends that you describe how you feel in a journal. Write down everything.

Stored anger and sadness are often associated with estrangement. Chopra suggests that after journaling you should try to talk to that person who has caused you pain. By expressing your desire to heal the relationship, by sharing your journal with them and reassuring the person whom you wrote about that you are not blaming them for your pain, there is a chance for healing the relationship.

Relationships can heal only if both parties want them to. If the other person rejects your attempt to heal the relationship, you can still take comfort in knowing that you did your part. By voicing your hurt or pain directly to the other person or in journal form, you will find closure regardless of the response from the person.

HOW DO DANGEROUS EMOTIONS DESTROY OUR LIVES?

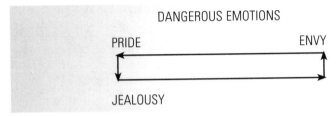

Low self-esteem and the absence of unconditional love are often at the root of jealousy. Jealousy is a very destructive emotion because it is self-defeating. You can only feel jealous when you believe that someone or something else is having, doing, being or withholding someone that you desire. Jealousy is founded on the false idea that God has supplied only a limited amount of love or good in this world. If you deeply believe this, you will naturally become jealous of the restricted amount of what you desire. The truth is that God gives you abundance, which is yours just by asking Him in faith.

In addition, when you learn to love yourself unconditionally, your self-esteem and confidence become impregnable. You will realize that there is nothing to be jealous about. You will be able to accept and love others without fear or envy. "Perfect love casts out fear" (1 John 4:18, NKJV).

When you see a friend or acquaintance achieve or acquire something wonderful in life, be happy and thankful for them. Any feelings of jealousy will only hurt and retard your progress.

PRIDE

Low self-esteem produces false pride, envy, anger, prejudice, resentment and arrogance. These personality traits may be labeled as pride, but in fact they are pride turned inside out. Any exercise in false pride may harm another and always hurts the person misusing his or her proud nature.

False pride is usually born out of fear, self-doubt and anger. The person becomes heavily burdened with fear and self-doubt and angrily rebels against these traits by adopting a superior attitude.

True self-confidence is a healthy mixture of faith, self-control, compassion, achievement, purpose and love. As a child of God, you cannot help but be self-confident of all that you are in Him and all that you are becoming through His help.

ENVY

Low self-esteem and an unforgiving, resentful nature are associated with envy. Envy and resentment can keep you trapped in a life that prevents you from God's abundance. Your thoughts can make you poor and unhappy. The surest way to become poor in spirit and in your pocketbook is to be envious of others. Envy is an enemy to success in life and causes a multitude of problems, most of them to the person who is envious. Building your self-confidence daily will gradually replace all of the life-destroying effects that envy brings upon your mind, body and spirit.

God made you a very special and unique expression of Him. No one else is just like you. You are valuable to God. Therefore, there is no reason for you to be envious of anyone or anything—because you have it all.

ANGER

One of the most dangerous of all emotions is anger. Unresolved anger is very serious and very destructive to your emotional and physical health. You can break free of unresolved anger. All that is required is insight into the causes of your anger.

When anger is not dealt with immediately, it festers within our souls, causing pain, isolation and eventually physical disease. Anger often stems from fear, frustration, hurt or a combination of all three.

> Do not let the sun go down on your anger.

The only regret I have is that I didn't grieve or vent my anger over my parent's divorce when it happened. At first I was actually relieved. I was in denial that it would affect me so profoundly. I was just relieved that the fighting was over and closure occurred. My mistake was that I tried to wear a smile and appear to be happy, sometimes overly so.

People commented about what a strong, resilient little girl I was. My teacher marveled at my need for perfection and excellence when it came to class work, artwork, science projects and anything else I tackled. I did this to feel accepted and appreciated. Down deep inside this little girl was really hurting. Little did I realize that this hurt would prove a catalyst to a life of self-discovery.

My parent's divorce catapulted me into early adulthood. I realize now that if I had been allowed to be a little girl just a little longer I could have cried and released the pain and might not have suffered such severe emotional depletion as an adult.

I now have no anger in connection to my parent's divorce. I do know now, however, that their breakup and dysfunction were the root cause of my emotional pain. But once again, being better, not bitter, is the key.

If you have struggled with deep hurts, here's my advice. Release, release, release! Let out your emotions, and allow yourself to feel them and then let go. Suppressing your emotions year after year leads to anger—one of the most dangerous emotions.

Listed below are the ten warning signs of anger. See if you can relate to any of the signs. If so, anger could be playing a big part in your emotional or physical health. With the realization of hidden anger comes release.

TEN WARNING SIGNS OF ANGER

- Overly critical
- Low self-esteem
- Divorced parents
- Can't get close to people
- Overly controlling
- Blame others for mistakes
- Untrusting
- Confrontational
- Overreact
- Parents indifferent toward you or not supportive

If a tree is hit with lightning, it may be completely unharmed. Or the damage it suffers can range from minor to severe. If a rain-drenched tree is hit by lightening, chances are it will not be injured because the moisture on the outside of the tree will conduct the lightning along the outside to the ground. On the other hand, if the tree is dry and has a wet dead area inside the trunk, it could literally explode, slinging branches and propelling pieces of wood as far as one hundred feet. This happens because the lightning travels rapidly down the moist interior of the tree, heating it to a very high temperature in thousandths of a second.

Isn't this a good illustration of the explosiveness of a fiery temper? Like a tree with a rotten heart struck by lightning, when you begin to boil inside, harm will come to you. That's why the psalmist said, "Refrain from anger and turn from wrath; do not fret—it leads only to evil" (Ps. 37:8). And Paul warned, "Let all bitterness, and wrath, and anger…be put away from you" (Eph. 4:31, KJV). Again he said, "But now ye also put off all these; anger, wrath…" (Col. 3:8, KJV). Like the tree blazing inside, "wrath kills a foolish man" (Job 5:2, NKJV).

As lightning strikes in the same place more than once, so "a man of great wrath will suffer punishment; for if you rescue him, you will have to do it again" (Prov. 19:19, NKJV). His anger will continue to get him in trouble, and he will have to be rescued over and over.

According to *Strong's Exhaustive Concordance of the Bible,* the Greek root for the word *wrath* means "to sacrifice, kill, slaughter." Like lightning traversing the inside of a tree, wrath can boil up inside a person in an instant and even bring about death. Like the tree in which the lightning travels, a person filled with wrath or anger is apt to explode. The Bible puts it this way: "Anger rests in the bosom of fools" (Eccles. 7:9, NKJV).

> The greatest remedy for anger is delay.
>
> —LUCIUS ANNEUS SENECA

Do you have differences with anyone? Do all in your power to make those differences right before the charges build, the situation explodes and what took years to build is destroyed in a moment.

- Learn to control your emotions.
- Do not overreact.
- Take responsibility for your own emotional self.
- There are *no* emotional saviors.
- Forgive once and for all.
- Surround yourself with positive, uplifting people.
- Pray and read the Bible daily. Ask God to change your heart.
- Read only uplifting publications and listen to uplifting music.
- Monitor your thoughts and words. Speak life! The power of life and death are in the tongue.[2]

BITTERNESS

Now comes the conscious choice. You can choose to hold on to your hurt or pain and grow increasingly bitter, or you can deal with it, release it and feel better. My own brother is a dramatic illustration of this. We both lived in the same home growing up. Both of us are the products of my parent's divorce. He became bitter, not all at once, mind you, but over the course of his life. He assumed the victim role early on in his life, and the victim he certainly became.

He was an angry child and teen. In adulthood, his anger, resentment and blaming nature paralyzed his life so much so that he turned to drugs and alcohol. Although he overcame his drug and alcohol habit, he is still unable to trust, a feeling rooted in his childhood. As a result, he is unable to form lasting and meaningful relationships.

The difference for you will be how you choose to react. Long ago I chose to be a survivor. I am writing this book as a testimony to the fact that bitter is definitely not better. I experienced loss, and I forgave, released and loved. Today I am truly grateful because I am better for it.

FORGIVENESS

Here is a mental exercise that I learned years ago on my journey to emotional wellness. I found it to be quite powerful when it came to seeing just how much we all have in common. We all need love. There are no exceptions. The first time I did this "forgiveness exercise," I cried like a baby. It released a lot of painful emotions that were associated with my father's lack of involvement in my life. If you cry, know that you are experiencing a release. Old hurts are rising to the top and are being expelled.

Let's begin. Picture a large stage. On that stage, picture the person or persons who hurt you or who did not love you or abandoned you. Next, shrink that person or persons down to their childhood size. See them as little children, lonely, scared and needing to be loved. Hold on to that vision for just a moment. Realize that we all are little children deep inside.

Now, tell that little child or the children on the stage that you love them and forgive them. Then shrink them even smaller in your mind, and put them into a mental pocket just over your heart. Keep them safe and think of them lovingly each day. When I did this exercise and put my father in my pocket, I understood that he did all that he knew how to do. I no longer took it personally. The following words came to me: "Father, forgive them; for they know not what they do" (Luke 23:34, KJV).

I learned that many of our hurts and much of our emotional pain is made worse when we believe that others deliberately wronged us. In some cases, it may be true. But in most cases, people are so busy with their own lives that they simply have no time to purposely cause hurt and pain to others. Much of the emotional pain we experience is unintentionally inflicted upon us.

Forgiveness literally short-circuits a cascade of stress hormones that accelerates heart rate, shuts down the immune system and encourages blood clotting. But unforgiveness and holding on to anger increases your chance of a heart attack fivefold! It also increases your risk of cancer, high blood pressure, high cholesterol and a host of chronic diseases.

As I mentioned earlier, forgiveness is a decision you ultimately have to make. You must consciously choose to give up your feelings of unforgiveness and anger. While anger and resentment are perfectly natural responses to situations that hurt or upset you, you cannot run the risk of letting negative experiences affect your attitude about people or life in general. If you do, it will leave you open to emotional health robbers such as anxiety, depression, poor self-esteem and staying in the victim role.

Forgiving is not necessarily forgetting. It is unrealistic to think that you can forget about an injustice, hurt or wound inflicted upon you by someone you love. You do have a memory, and the memory will always be with you. Forgiving is letting go of the anger and hurt attached to it and moving on with your life. Forgiving results in better sleep, increased feelings of love, more ability to trust and the eradication of physical symptoms that are connected to the anger or unforgiveness.

Forgiveness researcher Robert Enright, PhD, professor of educational psychology at the University of Wisconsin at Madison, developed the following quiz known as the "Enright Forgiveness Inventory." This abbreviated version will help you to determine whether or not you have truly forgiven someone who has hurt you. If after scoring yourself you discover that you have not completely forgiven, then ask God to help you to forgive once and for all. Go into prayer and turn the situation over in faith. Prayer could be your missing piece of the forgiveness puzzle.[3]

QUIZ: HOW FORGIVING ARE YOU?

Directions: Think about a specific person and what he or she has done. Focus on the most recent injustice. Then answer a, b or c by circling the number next to the answer that represents how you feel about the person who has hurt you.

Key: SD = strongly disagree   D = disagree
A = agree   SA = strongly agree

1. The best description of my feelings is that I:
    a. resent him or her   (SD–4, D–3, A–2, SA–1)
    b. dislike him or her   (SD–4, D–3, A–2, SA–1)
    c. love him or her   (SD–4, D–3, A–2, SA–1)

2. When I think about the person I:
    a. wish him or her well   (SD–4, D–3, A–2, SA–1)
    b. think kindly about him or her (SD–4, D–3, A–2, SA–1)
    c. do not respect the person at all (SD–4, D–3, A–2, SA–1)

3. If given the opportunity, I would:
    a. return his or her phone call   (SD–4, D–3, A–2, SA–1)

b. put the person down   (SD−4, D−3, A−2, SA−1)

c. try to be helpful   (SD−4, D−3, A−2, SA−1)

SCORING:

Total your points and compare below.

- **9−12 points**: You're not forgiving the person; perhaps you are still angry. I recommend prayer.
- **13−20 points**: You're not forgiving, but you are moving in the direction of forgiveness. I believe that prayer will help the process.
- **21−26 points**: You are in transition to forgiveness. I firmly believe that prayer will make the transition smoother.
- **27−36 points**: You are forgiving. You guessed it. I recommend prayer in this case also. Thank God for the victory over the hurt and pain.[4]

According to Bernie S. Siegel, MD, in his famous book *Peace, Love, and Healing,* your body is the outward manifestation of your mind, and peace of mind is what you want to manifest.[5] When you value yourself, you express all your feelings, and then you let them go. What is most liberating is that by letting people know who you are and where you are in life means that fewer conflicts occur. Relationships improve, and even your business improves. If you are uncomfortable about expressing anger, think of it as righteous indignation, which even Jesus displayed. Anger, anxiety, depression, fear and other emotions are dangerous if they remain buried inside, unexpressed and not dealt with.[6]

KEY TO YOUR EMOTIONAL SELF

As I mentioned earlier, dangerous emotions can play a part in the development of disease. Your emotional self is the center or core of your life. It helps you to express love and compassion. It also helps you to feel hurt and pain. God intended for us to be emotional beings, not just physical ones. It is our emotions that allow us to enjoy joyful, fulfilling and heartfelt relationships with others. The emotional self allows us to feel life from our heart center.

Life without emotional connections is empty, boring and a depressing existence. Once people experience hurt, rejection, abandonment and pain, they tend to stuff these dangerous emotions. When the emotional self is overloaded and out of balance, your physical, mental and spiritual life suffers. The simple fact that you are reading this book indicates that you have a natural desire to bring all areas of your life into balance. When balance is achieved, you can then be the ultimate expression of what God wants you to be.

To effectively deal with and heal your emotional pain once and for all, you need to find the root of your pain. When I design a program for a client who has health challenges, I try to find the root cause. Once I identify the cause, I address it with herbs, vitamins, detoxification and the like. Healing then follows and is complete. The same holds true for the emotional self.

THREE SOURCES OF EMOTIONAL PAIN

In Kevin Lane Turner's book *A Journey to the Other Side of Life,* he states that there are three sources or roots of emotional pain. They are wounding, unfulfilled emotional expectations and habits that result from wounding and unfulfilled expectations. Let's dissect them.

WOUNDING

A wounding is a hurt that was inflicted upon you by someone whom you loved or cared for. This wounding either betrayed you or violated you. A wounding could have been a major one-time event or a series of woundings throughout your life. The pain of a wounding generally has been with you a long time deep inside your core or heart.

UNFULFILLED EXPECTATIONS

This is when you look to a person, relationship, job or project to work out in a certain way. The problem begins when it does not turn out the way you planned or expected, and the disappointment drains you emotionally. This often happens after a divorce or when any other relationship ends.

Many times we are guilty of placing demands, desires, emotional hopes and dreams on those closest to us in order to feel loved and accepted. This really isn't fair. It only pressures those closest to us and results in their pulling away. Then come the feelings of rejection, which add another straw to the camel's back.

HABITS

Habits are the third source of emotional pain. Because of wounding and unfulfilled emotional expectations, we acquire negative habits that hinder us from overcoming the pain that torments our hearts. Emotional pain that is not dealt with affects the way we react on a daily basis. Emotional pain can cause habits that make us think, say, feel and do things that are not really a reflection of our true selves. This then sets us up for even more pain and makes us feel guilty, weak, like a bad person and inferior.

How do you heal and overcome the wounding and get back to your old self again? Volumes have been written on this topic. The self-help industry is booming because of all the hurting people out there.

It has been said that the power unleashed by your emotional self is far greater than the power of your body. When you are depleted from wounding, anxiety, stress or pain, your emotional self becomes so powerful that it can make you physically do, say and think things that you normally would not. When you are replenished and balanced, your emotional self becomes an outlet for you to express love, happiness and peace.

So, how do you get a grip back on years of wounding and depletion? The answer is simple; you must understand your feelings. You must learn how your emotional self works.

We have already discussed brain depletion and restoration using amino acids. We looked at this first because after the brain is replenished, it's easier to heal the emotional self.

The second step in healing your emotional self is to learn to control your emotions. Now remember, emotions are powerful. You can't harness them, but you can learn to control your emotional response. Forgiving the people or situations that have wounded you will do this. This will release your heart and you will be able to experience love and peace.

Next, you must change the way you react or, in many cases, overreact to those around you. Monitor your thoughts and your words. Begin to speak goodness and life to all with whom you come into contact. It may be necessary to change your circle of friends. Are your friends negative, complaining, draining and unsupportive? Then my question to you is, *Are they really friends?* You need to take the steps necessary to strengthen *yourself* emotionally. You will find that as you change your internal dialogue, God will bring new, more positive, uplifting, supportive friends into your life.

> For as he thinketh in his heart, so is he.
> —PROVERBS 23:7, KJV

As I was listening to the radio late one night, I began focusing intently on the lyrics in every song. I found a common thread—"How can I live without you?" "How am I supposed to live without you?" "Can't live, if living is without you." "If you leave me now, you'll take away the very heart of me." These types of lyrics are common in our society. These lyrics reflect how we feel in general these days; we look to others to give us a sense of belonging, self-worth and confidence. This can be dangerous. Too many people are more concerned about *getting* than *giving*. When you seek an "emotional savior outside yourself," you will always come up short, and your feelings of value and self-worth will only diminish. This is why you must come to the place in your life where you have forgiven and released fear, anger, grief and wounding before you become victorious. It is only then that you can have a healthy, full life. Everything good and positive will flow to you when you are healed and emotionally restored. It is a wonderful state of being. You must take responsibility for your own emotional healing. No one else can do it for you. God can strengthen you so you can walk through the muck and mire of old pain and trauma. As you walk through it, rest in God; He will bring you through it!

A MESSAGE TO WOMEN

Many women invest their whole lives in a man, whether it be their husband or boyfriend. While it is true that a man can be your lover and companion, he cannot be your lord. A man cannot heal your pain and hurt. Men need healing, too. Both men and women need to take their pain, fear, grief, unforgiveness and unresolved issues of anger to the Lord. Men and women together can seek God as their source for healing. As T. D. Jakes says in his book *The Lady, Her Lover and Her Lord,* "We may be each other's nurses or assistants, but we cannot perform the surgery. We all are, at best, just helpers. The detailed craftsmanship must come from the Master."

He goes on to say that God is the great comforter. "He can unravel the dark shroud of grief and release the captive heart that is buried within. He has the ability to wipe away trauma and restore peace. He catches our tears and collects our pains."[7]

Sometimes the difficulties we experience are a part of God's shaping and molding our lives.

CHAPTER 9

A Work
in Progress

God is the Potter and we are the clay. He molds and shapes us. Just when we think He's done, He fires us in the kiln of life. Sometimes we feel that the heat is so intense we think we'll explode. Only then does He take us out of the fire and cool us with His love. When He's through, He puts us on display for the entire world to see. We're a new creation with a brand-new chance at a life that has been restored from a once-broken vessel.

Never be afraid to take your dangerous emotions to God. He is calling you to do so.

RELEASE THY GRIEF

My child, lean thy head upon My bosom. Well I know thy weariness, and every burden I would lift. Never bury thy griefs, but offer them up to Me. Thou wilt relieve thy soul of much strain if ye can lay every care in My hand. Never cling to any trouble hoping to resolve it thyself, but turn it over to Me; and in doing so ye shall free Me to work it out.[1]

People who believe in a compassionate God take comfort from that and have a sense of control when things go wrong.[2]

LIGHT AT THE END OF THE TUNNEL

While writing this book, I encountered a prime example of how dangerous emotions coupled with brain and body depletion can ruin a life. A man came to my home to repair some plumbing. He was clearly not himself. He was racing around, sweating and wringing his hands. He had been to my home many times in the past, but on this particular day I knew he was in trouble emotionally and physically. I asked him if he was all right, and all of a sudden the floodgates opened. He began to tell me how his wife just served him with divorce papers after twenty-eight years of marriage. She was his best friend, so he felt betrayed. In addition, he had no family in the area except for his three children, who were now living with his wife.

The thoughts of being without his children deeply hurt him. To make matters worse, he shared with me that his wife always put him down and always complained about finances while he worked harder and harder to please her. When it came to sleeping, he told me he only slept about two or three hours a night! He ate only one meal a day, which was dinner. He was lonely, tired, distraught and even questioned if there was a God. The saddest thing he shared with me was that he was thinking about ending it all. He felt lonely, isolated, betrayed, angry, disillusioned, cheated and mentally, physically, emotionally and spiritually drained.

I told him that God knew the pain he was going through. I encouraged him to let the Lord keep him through this time and to rest in Him. Next, I recommended that he read any of Billie J. Salhey's books on anxiety and emotional fatigue. I educated him on how the brain becomes depleted from unrelenting stress, poor diet, not enough sleep, grief, anger and just about any of the emotions he was feeling.

I recommended that he try GABA, magnesium, liquid serotonin and an herbal anxiety formula. In addition, the tape series Attacking Anxiety and Depression from the Midwest Center for Stress and Anxiety would help him understand why he felt the way he did and why his body and mind were so out of control. He thanked me and told me that he hoped I was right, because he didn't think that he could hold on much longer. I looked at him and softly told him that God is good and is faithful. With that he left.

Three weeks after my first encounter with my repairman I am happy to report that he seems to be doing much better! He shared with me that after taking his GABA, magnesium, liquid serotonin and anxiety herbal formula, he slept through the night for the first time in months.

The following morning he drove to a restaurant and ordered a large breakfast. This was a dramatic improvement because previously he could only eat one meal a day, usually at the end of the day. If he tried to eat anything before then, he would become ill. He also seems in better spirits and is filled with hope. He now sees a light at the end of the tunnel. Sometimes that's enough.

DANGEROUS EMOTIONS NEWS FLASH

According to Tedd Mitchell, MD, director of the Cooper Clinic's Wellness Program in Dallas, Texas, research has found the following:

1. *Being lonely can be risky.* People without a strong connection to family, friends or groups were four to six times more apt to die according to a six-year study, regardless of the health, wealth, race, activity or use of health services.[3]
2. *Talking down.* Older women who did not talk to others about their problems had higher blood pressure than the ones who did talk.
3. *Marriage perks.* Married people live longer, eight to ten years for men, three to four years for women. Divorced men have the highest death rate.
4. *Love hurts so good.* Men who said their wives didn't show them love were twenty times more apt to develop chest pain than men with loving wives.
5. *Mommy and daddy.* Ninety-one percent of men without a warm childhood relationship with their mothers developed serious disease in midlife. In addition, men

had an 82 percent chance of serious disease in midlife without a warm relationship with dad.

6. *Let go and let God.* People who did not participate in social groups and did not draw comfort from religion were seven times more likely to die within six months of major surgery.

POSITIVE EMOTIONS TO GROW ON

THE SERENITY PRAYER

God grant me the *serenity* to accept the things I cannot change;
The *courage* to change the things I can;
And the *wisdom* to know the difference.

—REINHOLD NIEBUHR

Sometimes the paths we take are long and hard, but, always remember, those hard paths are the ones that lead to most beautiful views.

—COLLIN McCARTY

Getting rid of negative emotions is not enough. We must learn to substitute positive emotions in the spaces formerly occupied by the negative emotions.

TRUST

It is a trust that
If I fail now—
I shall not fail forever;
And if I am hurt,
I shall be healed.

—ANONYMOUS

Look at doubt and fear and keep in mind that your struggle is helping you to grow in faith! You are not alone at all; God is walking beside you in spirit and will be there with you to give you new strength, new peace and renewed happiness—all in His divine timing. Treat yourself as you would a friend. Encourage yourself.

Think only good thoughts. Be kind to yourself because kindness nurtures your soul.

Faith

Hold on to your faith as though it were a path to follow or a song you love to sing!

Overcoming

Emotional recovery is all about letting go of the high expectation of perfection that you have placed upon yourself and others. It is learning to love and accept yourself and others unconditionally. You can choose to be hopeless or hopeful. You can choose to act from faith rather than react from fear. Then you can enjoy life rather than barely survive it.

EMOTIONS TRANSLATE INTO THE PHYSICAL

In the book *Freedom through Health,* Terry Shepherd Friedmann, MD, agrees that one important aspect of raising the vitality of a person is to remove negative and emotional mental patterns that they have acquired and replace them with positive, creative patterns. He believes that until this concept is addressed fully, diseases cannot be completely reversed, nor can the patient be completely healthy.

Dr. Friedmann also discovered, as did I, that negative emotional patterns such as fear, anger, hatred, envy and resentment suppress the health of the body, mind and spirit. In other words, people are sick mentally, physically and spiritually simultaneously.[4]

One example of how negative emotions translate into physical disease is arthritis. Some studies have shown that persons who are fixed or rigid in their thoughts and behavior patterns are most often plagued with arthritis, the theory being that rigidity in thoughts creates inflexibility in the body. It also follows that pent-up emotions with resultant stress create high blood pressure, which stems from unrelieved internal pressure. Persons who have a hard time expressing love and other very personal feelings have blocked coronary arteries. Cancer seems to be connected to being disconnected, lonely or having a fear of loss.

Take, for example, families that have faced incredible hardship—whether it is from a death, divorce, job loss or financial ruin. One member of the family may suffer disease as a result of the stress, strain and subsequent immune suppression. Yet another member of that same family emerges unscathed and totally healthy. The difference appears to be in the attitudes of the two different family members.

Many of our physical and emotional problems revolve around our inability to release old, suppressed past hurts. This emotional injury from years ago can lodge in the region of the body that most relates to a specific emotion. For example, love has a connection to the heart region, breast region or bladder region, also known as the giving regions of the body. If we do not forgive and surrender our hurts, pain and anger, over a period of time the body literally starts taking it out on itself. I personally have experienced this phenomenon. Anger, fear and guilt are three of the most destructive emotions. They block the natural, harmonious flow of life and lead us down the path to disease and emotional breakdown.

Why me?

In the beginning I wondered if I would ever make it through the sadness, emptiness, pain and grief I was experiencing. These were times when I wondered, *Why me?* Then the sun began to peek out from between the clouds, and I could see beyond them.

As each ray of sunlight made its way back into my life, a new friendship was formed. I have a better understanding of my life and myself. I look back on my time in the valley as a period of growth.

Nothing wastes more time than worrying.

The longer one carries a problem, the heavier it becomes and the more it weighs you down.

Do not take things seriously, live a life of serenity, not a life of regrets.

Do not forget even for a minute...how very special you are to God.

—Unknown

140

PEEL YOUR ONION

Each one of us must deal with our own emotional demons. As you love, forgive and release the old patterns and tapes, think of it as peeling an onion. As you peel the old hurt away one layer at a time, your life will unfold and take on new meaning. As you peel away each layer, you will find that sweet internal part that is healthy, an inner core that is vibrant and free of illness. Once you return to that core place, you will now be able to choose to change with God's help as you react to future negative emotions.

Now consciously choose to handle your emotions with joy. Joy is the result of finding that inner peace once again. Your healed life will be good to the core.

THE GOLDEN YEARS ARE TRULY GOLDEN

Researchers at Fordham University in New York say that as you get older you'll get happier. They believe that this higher level of well-being may be partly explained by the fact that golden-agers are less likely to spend time with people that they don't get along with or simply do not like, thereby avoiding the stress. Maybe it's just being older and wiser.[5]

GIGGLES ARE GOOD!

LAUGHTER LOWERS STRESS

Evidence accumulated over the years suggests that laughter lowers stress hormones, blood pressure and pain as it boosts immunity. It's now twenty-four years since the famous author Norman Cousins first declared that funny movies should be a part of every patient's treatment. Today hundreds of hospitals have special rooms solely dedicated to humor. Some have visiting clown programs. The greater the trauma, it seems, the deeper the need to laugh. As a matter of fact, one of the first speakers to address an assembly at Columbine High School after the shootings was humorist Craig Zablocki.[6]

The importance of humor is now fact. Once you learn to use a few simple techniques, even the most high-strung among us will calm down. Most of us have a person or persons with whom we can have a good belly laugh. Maybe it's your best friend, your wife or husband, your children or coworkers. Whoever can share a laugh with you is blessing your mind and body with health. When you laugh, think of all the good chemicals that are being released to work in your body. Laughter costs you nothing but contributes much!

The American Film Institute has listed several dozen suggestions that are guaranteed to get you laughing. For more information, log on to the institute's Web site at www.afi.com/tvevents/100years/laughs/aspx. You will find "America's one hundred top funny movies" along with plot summaries and cast listings. I have listed some of the top fifteen knee-slappers for you:

- *Tootsie* (1982)
- *Dr. Strangelove* (1964)
- *Annie Hall* (1977)
- *Duck Soup* (1933)
- *Blazing Saddles* (1974)
- *M*A*S*H* (1970)
- *It Happened One Night* (1934)
- *Airplane!* (1980)
- *The Producers* (1968)
- *A Night at the Opera* (1935)
- *Young Frankenstein* (1974)
- *Bringing Up Baby* (1938)
- *The Philadelphia Story* (1940)

CHAPTER 10

Reach Out
to Others

Not only is laughter the best medicine, but friendship is also. An entire new wave of studies shows the power of social connections. Positive relationships are crucial for your mental and physical well-being, and the absence of these life-enhancing relationships is very detrimental. Researchers are learning that the ties that bind are also the bonds that heal.

The better part of one's life consists of his friendships.

—ABRAHAM LINCOLN

THE HEALING
BALM OF ACCEPTANCE

According to Mark Leary, PhD, of Wake Forest University in Winston-Salem, North Carolina, longing for stable relationships is a fundamental human need that has only two requirements— regular contact and persistent demonstrations of caring. With every heartbeat we need to feel that we belong. The need for acceptance is built in, down to the marrow of our bones. In other words, friendship is not a luxury; it is a necessity. This is a good time to remember that Jesus is a "friend that sticks closer than a brother." (See Proverbs 18:24.)[1]

A friend is a flower in the garden of life.

—Unknown

New research is showing that women's immune systems suffer from a lack of connection and men's cardiovascular systems are affected by the lack of a close confidant. Loneliness can be lethal. The lack of positive social relationships can be a health hazard that encourages smoking, drinking, high blood pressure and a lack of exercise along with depression.

While it's true that modern technology may make life easier, it may also make it shorter. Science now says that people who have a lot of human contact can live twice as long as those who are isolated. Studies show that the fewer human connections we have at home, at work and in the community, the more likely we are to get sick, flood our brains with anxiety-causing chemicals and die prematurely. According to psychiatrist Edward M. Hallowell, MD, instructor in psychiatry at Harvard Medical School, "It's the unacknowledged key to emotional and physical health, and that's medical fact."

These days with divorce so common and job-jumping as a way of life, strong community involvement is lacking and an epidemic of isolation has emerged.

Oprah has a Gayle

Oprah Winfrey is one of the most successful women in television, and she is known the whole world over. She has built an empire and earns millions each year. Harpo, her production company, employs many talented people. She is influential and capable of making dreams come true for many who are not as privileged.

Oprah has become a household word, but I believe that Oprah would agree with me when I say that nothing—not fame, fortune and great influence—can take the place of the feeling of connectedness she shares with her best friend, Gayle King. I have watched Oprah interact with Gayle a few times on camera, and you can see how deep their friendship is and how much happiness they share because of it. It's as if there is an unspoken oath between them that promises to always be there for the other no matter what life brings.

Every one of us needs a Gayle in our life. Maybe yours is a childhood friend with whom you grew up and still keep in touch. Or maybe you have just met your best friend recently. What matters most is that you connect. A friendship is a heart connection that literally makes your heart sing, your emotional health soar and your physical health strong. It's one of the most powerful connections you can make in this life. If you have only one true friend in your life then you are wealthy indeed. Just ask Oprah and Gayle!

ARE YOU CONNECTED?

This self-test by Edward M. Hallowell, MD, will help you to discover how connected/adapted you are.

_____ Do you make time to be with members of your family even if it means giving up some activity you might enjoy?

_____ Do you eat family dinner together or spend time together each day?

_____ Do you know the people who live next door well enough to ask them to do a favor for you?

_____ Do you sometimes become so interested in your work that you forget what time it is or where you are?

_____ Do you know the details about your parents' or grandparents' lives?

_____ Are there special natural habitats that speak to you in ways that no other place can?

_____ Do you feel a connection to God?

_____ Do you feel OK about your body?

_____ Are you able to block useless information so that you are not overwhelmed?

_____ Do you have peace in your life?[2]

Obviously, the more yes answers you have, the more connected you are. Try focusing your attention on the areas in which you answered no. You'll be more connected and good to go!

ALL WORK AND WORRY AND NO PLAY LEAVE NOTHING BUT STRESS AT THE END OF THE DAY

When was the last time you allowed yourself to have fun? Those who deal with emotional pain and physical illness often seem to have a fun deficiency. This deficiency is very detrimental to your well-being. Some people are so stressed out that they can't even remember how to have fun. When I was going through years of emotional turmoil and illness, someone asked me what I did for fun. I was speechless. I couldn't even name one thing that I considered fun. I had forgotten how to have fun.

That one question really alerted me to the fact that I had better focus on fun as well as the other aspects of my life. You may be asking yourself, *FUN? What's that?*

To begin with, you must try to remember how you played or had fun in the past. Think back to your teens or twenties and analyze what it was you liked about the activities you used to enjoy. For example, were your activities planned or spontaneous? Were you a spectator or a participant?

Consider pastimes that differ from your work.

Make time for play. If you look closely at the lives of busy people, you'll notice that they always make time for what they need and want to do by planning it in their schedules. It's essential to fit playtime into your busy life.

Don't take your hobbies too seriously. This is hard for some type A personalities who are often too rigid in all that they undertake. If you approach your hobbies with rigid perfectionism, they will start to feel more like work than play.

SOOTHE YOUR BODY AND SOUL

It's time to treat yourself right. In this section you will learn some plain old common-sense advice to help you soothe your body and soul. When you treat yourself to some of these simple pleasures, your heart will be a little lighter. Think of them as preventative medicine against emotional depletion.

BOOST YOUR SELF-CONFIDENCE

Some people have a low self-image. If you find yourself always down in the dumps, you may need professional help from a therapist. But for the majority of people, small simple changes in their lives could have an enormous impact on their self-image.

Begin with a small change. Change your hairstyle or buy a new outfit or both. Take a friend with you for moral support and for fun. This will help to trigger a semiconscious thought process that will help you to think of yourself as more attractive, successful, capable and responsible. People generally believe that the better looking a person is, the better, smarter, more capable, responsible and nice he is. By looking good and carrying yourself more confidently, you will start feeling more confident.

Well-developed biceps can actually lift confidence levels in both men and women. Men, however, are more satisfied with themselves than their muscularly weaker peers. Women with greater upper body strength also have better self-esteem than those who are weaker.

Sticking to a regular workout routine also helps you to develop self-discipline, which will improve your self-esteem. Start an upward spiral of success with discipline and the confidence that arises from it. From there you will be emotionally capable of moving on to really big, tough changes that could make your life richer and more satisfying. You might decide to look for a better job, work on your relationship with your spouse or move to another part of the country and begin a whole new chapter in your life. Of course, these are major changes, but it has been said that a journey of a thousand miles begins with one simple step. With increased self- confidence and discipline, the journey can begin.

INVEST IN THE JOURNEY

First, accept yourself just the way you are. Be patient and gentle with yourself. People overcoming emotional depletion and low self-esteem often are very hard on themselves. Instead of beating yourself up, simply take steps to change what you do not like about your current situation.

Try not to swim upstream. Realize that there are some things in life that you cannot change. In these cases, change the way you perceive the troubling facts or situations.

Ask and you shall receive. Turn the things that you cannot

change over to God in prayer. Then begin to act as though the situation has become whatever you want it to be.

Learn a skill. Learning a new skill such as oil painting, quilting or photography will foster a sense of accomplishment, which is one of the best confidence boosters known.

Who are you right now? Write down a list of positive things about yourself each week. It may be hard at first because most people focus only on the negative things in their lives. It takes pulling hard in the positive direction to notice just how many wonderful and positive things you have in your life right now.

Substitute faith for fear

A few years ago I had a client named Mary. She was dealing with intense fear about her children's lives, her house payments, her health, her husband's fidelity, her ailing parents and more. Fear clearly was disrupting her life. After designing a nutritional health-building program for her, I recommended that she begin each day with a thirty-minute walk.

What started as a stress-relieving exercise routine turned into a life-changing spiritual experience for Mary. As she walked each morning she prayed. She prayed for her relationship with her husband, their finances and the health of her family members. As the days and weeks passed, she prayed for people in her neighborhood and friends who were struggling. She prayed for her business and direction in all that she undertook.

Mary's stress levels fell dramatically, her relationships became more fulfilling, her needs were provided for and she stopped feeling anxious because she had turned everything over to God in prayer. Add in the positive effect that walking had on her health, and the transformation was complete—body, mind and spirit.

Avoid anxiety

Take a look at seven dangerous habits of highly anxious people.

1. *Trying to be perfect.* People who feel that they're always failing can't help but be nervous wrecks. Perfectionism is a self-destructive, self-imposed stress. Nobody is perfect.

Learn to give yourself a break. Look for the positive side to every disappointing situation.

2. *Stuffing it.* Bottled-up emotion is often the root cause of anxiety. Anxiety may be a signal to you that you need to let your feelings out. Talk to a trusted friend and unburden yourself. If you don't have a friend with whom you feel comfortable enough to share, then write your feelings in a journal.

3. *It's not my fault.* Anxious people often feel they are responsible for the well-being and happiness of the entire world. As a result, when things go wrong they blame themselves. Learn to pay attention to your thoughts. Anxious, guilty thinking wears you out mentally and physically because you literally feel as if you have the weight of the world on your shoulders.

4. *All or none.* This is closely related to perfectionism. Try to eliminate the following words from your vocabulary— *never, always, must* and *should.* These words leave you little room for error in your day-to-day life. This will only set you up for failure.

5. *Jumping to conclusions.* Emotionally drained people usually have a low opinion of themselves and often think that others do as well. Don't jump to conclusions. You must stop living your life in someone else's head.

6. *I've got a secret.* Sometimes the cause of panic attacks and free-floating anxiety is personal secrets. It takes an incredible amount of mental energy to make sure that no one knows your secret. Try instead to share your secret with someone you can trust—a friend, relative, therapist or pastor.

7. *Playing ostrich.* Some worriers bury their heads in the sand until it is too late. If you are faced with a situation

149

or event that causes you anxiety, preparation is the key. If you're afraid of driving, take a friend along and make sure your car is in perfect working order. Map out your route so you don't get lost. These minor considerations can diffuse your fear about the situation.[3]

CHAPTER 11

Use the Emotional Recovery Action Plan

This workbook section will help you determine where you need to balance your life. It will also help you to form an outline to put your emotional recovery plan in action.

BALANCE YOUR LIFE

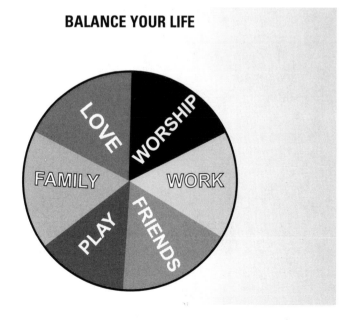

151

ONE—DETERMINE
IF YOUR LIFE IS BALANCED

Is your life out of balance? Answer the following questions carefully:

- Where do you spend most of your time?

- Where do you spend too little time?

- In order to balance your life, what areas do you need to focus on?

- What action will you take to bring the main areas of your life into balance?

TWO—MAKE EXERCISE
A REGULAR PART OF YOUR DAILY LIFE

Exercise is crucial for physical and emotional well-being. How do you measure up in this area?

- What form of exercise do you use?

- How many times a week do you exercise?

- How long do you exercise during each session?

- What type aerobic or cardiovascular exercise do you do?

- What kinds of weight training are in your daily routine?

THREE—RESOLVE
RELATIONSHIP ISSUES

It is also important to forgive and release all your feelings of hurt and wounding. Check off the following list of relationships that may have been affecting your emotional health. Then list the dangerous emotion that is connected to that relationship.

Mother	_____	Father	_____
Brother	_____	Sister	_____
Wife	_____	Husband	_____
Boss	_____	Coworker	_____
Child	_____		

In each case where you checked a relationship problem, a conscious effort must be made on your part to address the hurt, to forgive or ask for forgiveness and finally to heal the relationship. Let go once and for all!

FOUR—LEARN TO RELAX

Relax—you deserve it! Take time to relax. Make the following relaxation techniques a part of your daily life. Give yourself time to unwind, or you will remain tense or irritable. During relaxation the body repairs, de-stresses and rebuilds.

To relax, I will:

❏ Have a weekly massage
❏ Take a warm aromatherapy bath
❏ Relax with a good book
❏ Take a relaxing walk
❏ Pray or meditate
❏ Practice deep breathing or the MANTLE technique every night before bed
❏ Listen to soothing music

FIVE—RECOVER FROM STRESS
BY FEEDING YOUR BODY PROPERLY

To de-stress, I will:

❏ Watch my sugar intake
❏ Limit or eliminate caffeine
❏ Eliminate alcohol

❏ Eat whole, live foods and minimize processed foods
❏ Take dietary supplements that boost my body and brain function daily

SIX—FEED YOUR
MIND WITH POSITIVE FOOD

❏ Love unconditionally
❏ Forgive
❏ Use faith to banish fear
❏ Pray
❏ Allow yourself to read only uplifting materials

SEVEN—OUT WITH
THE OLD; IN WITH THE NEW

Get control of your life! Eliminate from your life the things that are not working, and focus on the things that are working. This will help to liberate you from frustration and stress.

Things that *are* working:

Personal Life	Business Life
_____	_____
_____	_____
_____	_____
_____	_____
_____	_____

Things that are *not* working:

Personal Life	Business Life
_____	_____
_____	_____
_____	_____
_____	_____
_____	_____

DO-IT-YOURSELF RELAXATION TAPE

Here's a great way to relax: Create your own relaxation tape. You will need the following supplies:

- One tape recorder
- One sixty-minute blank cassette tape suitable for voice recording
- Twenty to thirty minutes of your time

A homemade relaxation tape can be just as effective as any relaxation tape on the market. The benefit of making your own tape is that you can tailor it to your own particular tastes. The following *basic script* is yours to be creative with. If you know someone with a soothing voice, enlist him or her to read the basic script for you. Try adding background music. Record birds or waves lapping at the shore or anything that you feel will help you to achieve relaxation. Play your tape twice a day to start off. After a couple of weeks, play it once a day. Select a special time of day just for your relaxation tape and you. At first it may feel uncomfortable to relax. You have been so tightly wound for so long that letting go feels a little unsettling. This feeling will pass in time. When it does, it's a signal to you that you are making real progress.

RELAX TO THE MAX

Basic relaxation tape script:[1]

> [[Insert your name,]] this is your time to relax. Let go of all that you have been thinking about. Let go of all your worries. This time belongs to your body. Let your mind be at peace. You deserve it.
>
> This is your time to relax. Each time you relax fully, it will become easier and easier to feel deeply relaxed.
>
> Take a moment to settle yourself comfortably on a bed or sit up straight in a straight-backed chair. Slip off your shoes and loosen anything that is tight. (Pause for fifteen seconds.) Good.

Say to yourself, *I can relax now and breathe comfortably. This is my time to relax.* (Pause.)

Now take a deep, deep breath. Good. Hold it. Count silently to five. (Pause for five seconds.) Now, exhale, counting to ten as you do. (Pause for ten seconds.)

Let's try that again. Deep breath, hold it, count to five. (Pause five seconds.) Now release it, counting to ten as you exhale. (Pause for ten seconds.)

This third time, hunch your shoulders up as close to the ears as you can get them and hold yourself still. Count silently to five. (Pause five seconds.) Now, exhale, pushing all the air out of your lungs. Let yourself exhale slowly.

Good. This is your time to relax. Breathe deeply and slowly. Feel your breath expand your belly and then feel your belly sink back down as you exhale. Stay with this for a few minutes. (Pause for a few moments.)

Now, close your eyes.

In your mind's eye, concentrate on your feet. Inhale and at the same time tense your feet, curling your toes up. Hold the position while you silently count to six. (Pause for six seconds.)

Now exhale and relax your feet. Feel the exhalation leaving your feet. See how good it feels to let go. Inhale again and then exhale slowly while you say to yourself, *Gently relax, relax, relax.*

Now inhale and contract your calves. Make them as tight as you can. Good. Hold for a count of six. (Pause for six seconds.) Exhale slowly and relax the muscles. Experience how good that relaxation feels. Inhale and exhale slowly again. Say, *Relax; relax; relax.*

Now inhale and contract the muscles in your thighs. Hold for a count of six. (Pause for six seconds.) Excellent. Now exhale slowly. Focus on how wonderful that feels. Inhale again and exhale slowly. Say, *Relax, relax, relax.*

Now inhale and contract the muscles in your buttocks

and your stomach. Hold for a count of six. (Pause for six seconds.) Very good! Now exhale slowly. Enjoy the sensation. Feel the exhalation leave your buttocks and stomach. Take another breath and release it slowly. Say, *Relax; relax; relax.*

Now, do the same with your chest and breathing muscles. Contract your muscles and hold. Count to six. (Pause for six seconds.) Now exhale slowly. See how pleasurable this is. Feel the exhalation bathe your chest. Take another breath, and gently release it. Say, *Relax; relax; relax.*

Now it's time to focus on your shoulders and chest muscles. Tighten your shoulders by pulling them up and back. Contract the muscles and hold. Count silently to six. (Pause for six seconds.) Good! Now exhale slowly, letting all the tension drain away. This feels wonderful. Take another slow breath and then release it. Say, *Relax; relax; relax.*

Now inhale and tighten your neck and neck muscles. Hold while you silently count to six. (Pause for six seconds.) Exhale and release. Focus on the sensation. Inhale again and exhale slowly. Say, *Relax; relax; relax.*

Now do the same thing with the muscles in your arms, from your shoulders to fingertips. Inhale and contract your muscles. Tight; tighter! Hold for six. (Pause for six seconds.) Great! Exhale and relax your arm from the shoulders right down to the fingertips. Tune into how that feels. Take another slow breath. Exhale. Say, *Relax; relax; relax.*

Now inhale and tighten up your whole face. Tighter! Tighter, still! Hold it for a count of six. (Pause for six seconds.) That's good. Now exhale slowly and relax your face. Good. You feel great. Inhale again and then exhale. Say, *Relax; relax; relax.*

Now focus on your breath down in your belly. Feel your belly rise and fall with your breath. Stay with this until you feel even more deeply relaxed. (Pause for three minutes.)

Take a few minutes now to experience the deep sense

of relaxation. Make a mental note of this feeling so you can return to it whenever you need it.

Now calmly count backward from ten. When you reach one you will feel deeply relaxed and invigorated. 10...9...8...7...6...5...4...3...2...1. Open your eyes. Thank yourself for taking the time to relax. As the days and weeks go by you will find it easier to relax.

CONCLUSION

Now that you've seen how easy it is to replenish the brain and to renew the mind, let's look at some powerful strategies for rebuilding your body.

PART THREE
REBUILD

CHAPTER 12

Diffuse Your Emotional Time Bomb and Regain Your Health

In this section we will take an in-depth look at the most common illnesses that we face today, the possible emotional connections to those illnesses and the corresponding nutritional health-restoring protocol. Continue to follow the brain-restoring protocol outlined in part one as an insurance policy against future depletion. Remember that all illness has a mind/body connection. We will now focus on the body.

Let's discover the emotional link to the present condition of your physical health. By working on underlying emotions such as fear, anger and resentment, and by applying powerful healing principles listed, you can take an active roll in reclaiming your health.

Remember that your condition did not occur overnight. It took years upon years of hurt and trauma and of suppressing emotions mentally, physically and spiritually deep within you.

Healing begins with the realization of how great a part your emotions have played in the present level of your health. You must no longer deny that you are angry, hurt or resentful of something or someone. You now must acknowledge it. You must deal with it now if you are to heal.

Go into prayer and ask for forgiveness for anything that you may have done that has harmed another individual. More

161

importantly, forgive anyone who has harmed you.

Let it go! Let God take the past hurt from you. If you can't forgive, then you cannot be forgiven. Now you are ready to dive head-first into the ocean of emotion that will open into a sea of healing and relief.[1]

Let's look closely at the link between your emotions and your health.[2]

ANXIETY
UNDERLYING DANGEROUS EMOTION—FEAR

What costs billions of dollars and ruins lives? Anxiety. And it's on the rise. I've been a victim of anxiety to the max. This became crystal clear to me as I battled recurrent panic attacks. Anxiety has risen to America's number-one health problem. Experts say that the reason for our anxiety is the scary place and time in history in which we're living. Some day Congress may even consider a new bill to require insurance coverage for several types of anxiety disorders. Click on the Internet to the Anxiety Disorders Association of America, and you will join the over 21.6 million Americans who have sought help from the Web site.

Anxiety is the result of physical and emotional stress that we encounter from day to day as the result of financial problems, relationship problems and nutrient deficiencies. The underlying dangerous emotion is fear.

A person experiencing anxiety may suffer from any or all of the following symptoms—shortness of breath, dizziness, colitis, insomnia, irritability, head, neck and backaches, panic attacks and high blood pressure, just to name a few.

The odds of your developing an anxiety disorder have doubled in the past four decades according to a study by the World Health Organization. The effects of anxiety are devastating. This is especially true if you are a teen with your whole future ahead of you. It's common for anxiety sufferers to develop such extreme avoidance behavior that they live limited lives, pass up careers and deny friendships. Some anxiety sufferers are unable to work or never get married. Eventually persons with untreated anxiety can become completely housebound. This is tragic because they can never recapture the time that they spent isolated and imprisoned by this invisible health robber.

People with anxiety disorders seem to have memories of trauma or frightening events imprinted on their brains. Their bodies seem to remain primed to respond with fear to whatever triggered the initial anxiety.

According to David H. Barlow, PhD, of the Center for Anxiety and Related Disorders at Boston University, people with anxiety disorders receive mental false alarms. Scientists do not understand what triggers the false alarms in anxiety-ridden individuals. They speculate that it is a complex mix of genetics, brain chemistry and psychology. Some studies point to a hereditary connection.

Researchers at the National Institute of Mental Health Center in Rockville, Maryland are gathering evidence that brain chemicals may function abnormally in a chronically anxious individual. Some studies are exploring early childhood experiences. The approaches to overcoming anxiety are as varied as the theories seem to be.

As you read earlier, the medication route offers pills to interrupt the chain of signals that sets up the anxiety reaction. These are the antidepressants. These drugs are commonly used with cognitive behavior to break the false alarm reactions and avoidance behaviors.

As you read on, you will learn of an amazing but logical approach to restore your brain, mind and body. For me it was the way back from the living hell of anxiety and emotional collapse. Keep in mind that while I do not profess to be a psychologist or therapist, I do say that I am an educator on nutrition and depletion in the body. My mission is to educate, encourage and help you to find your pathway to healing. I have experienced everything contained within these pages. I was the patient before I became the doctor. I can tell you from my own experience and educational background that the information will be life-changing and will help you build your mind, body and spirit to a new renewed level.

GABA and magnesium, as well as tyrosine, are antistress amino acids and minerals that act as calmers and balancers. People who suffer from anxiety need neurotransmitters to restore their brain's chemistry. Amino acids create needed neurotransmitters. You may also want to try Bach's Rescue Remedy (as noted earlier) when you are feeling tense and anxious.

Nutritional guidelines for overcoming anxiety are as follows: Avoid sugar, artificial sweetener, colas, caffeine, nitrates and fast foods. Avoid smoking, alcohol and coffee because they rob the body of B vitamins, which act as natural tranquilizers. The following comfort foods eaten at some time during the day can prevent nighttime panic attacks—brown rice, oatmeal, oat bran, a protein shake or mashed potatoes.

Deep breathing is also of great benefit to the anxious person. I personally practice deep breathing daily. Deep diaphramatic breathing is essential for stress relief, weight loss and increased energy. It costs so little and the oxygen is free. Systematic deep breathing diffuses stress and quells anxiety.

Anxiety can affect the famous and not so famous, rich, poor, young or old. With the numbers on the rise, anxiety knows no boundaries, touching the lives of many Americans.

MEDICAL DISORDERS AND ANXIETY

The following medical disorders may provoke anxiety symptoms. Check each one that you have experienced.

CARDIOVASCULAR

- ❏ Cardiac arrhythmia
- ❏ High blood pressure
- ❏ Mitral valve prolapse
- ❏ Congestive heart failure
- ❏ Heart attack

ENDOCRINE

- ❏ Hypoglycemia
- ❏ Cushing's syndrome
- ❏ Hyperthyroidism
- ❏ Carcnoid syndrome

RESPIRATORY

- ❏ Hyperventilation
- ❏ Emphysema
- ❏ Asthma
- ❏ Hypoxia

NEUROLOGICAL

- ❏ Vertigo
- ❏ Wilson's disease
- ❏ Migraine headaches
- ❏ Chronic pain
- ❏ Epilepsy

WHAT DOES THE BIBLE SAY ABOUT STRESS, FEAR AND ANXIETY?

Therefore I tell you, do not be anxious about your life, what you shall eat or what you shall drink, nor about your body, what you shall put on. Is not life more than food and the body more than clothing? Look at the birds of the air: they neither sow nor reap nor gather into barns, and yet your heavenly Father feeds them. Are you not of more value than they? And which of you by being anxious can add one cubit to his span of life?...

Therefore, do not be anxious, saying, "What shall we eat?" or "What shall we drink?" or "What shall we wear?" For the Gentiles seek all these things; and your heavenly Father knows that you need them all...Therefore do not be anxious about tomorrow, for tomorrow will be anxious for itself. Let the day's own trouble be sufficient for the day.

—MATTHEW 6:25–27, 31–32, 34, RSV

The Bible teaches us that we should not be anxious, fearful or stressed if we put our faith and trust in Christ. If you are dealing with stress and anxiety in your life, read these scriptures daily. Jesus lived in a stressful time that was filled with fear and anxiety. How did Jesus deal with His anxious moments? He knew how to carry everything to His Father and leave it there.

God is your Father also. Every day go to the Father in confidence and prayer when you are anxious, fearful or stressed. The Word of God will sustain you more than any health food, vitamin or herbal program. God will keep your mind from anxiety, fear and stress if you commune with Him daily.

God is in charge; He is on the throne. Carry your troubles to Him. He's waiting, so make the choice to believe and to walk in the will of the Father. He will demonstrate His love for you. People who suffer from anxiety seem to feel all alone and hopeless. He will be there to protect you, guide you and give you His peace. He is right beside you always, and He has your best interest at heart.

ARTHRITIS
UNDERLYING EMOTION—FEELING UNLOVED

The causes of arthritic diseases vary from emotional resentments to lifestyle, wear and tear, viruses and bacterial invasion. Approximately fifty million Americans suffer with one or more of the following arthritic conditions–gout, lupus, ankylosing spondylitis and rheumatism. Natural therapies, including lifestyle changes, do work very well. Again, going to the root cause is mandatory while addressing the pain and discomfort.

In order to reduce inflammation, the following supplements have been used with great success; Enzymedica's Purify digestive enzymes, 500–750 milligrams of bromelain between meals, DLPA to ease pain, 500–1,000 milligrams MSM. To repair and rebuild the joints, use glucosamine chondroitin, 500 milligrams of CMO and essential fatty acids. Adrenal health must also be addressed. Adrenal glandular supplement (I recommend Core Level Adrenal by Nutri-West of Florida), Royal Jelly and B complex are suggested. As a topical application, try Dr. Janet's Balanced by Nature Glucosamine Cream.

Follow my recommended eating plan. Make sure to have a green drink each day. (I recommend Kyo-Green.) Try to avoid the nightshade plants because they have been known to trigger arthritis symptoms in a large percentage of sufferers. They are peppers, eggplants, tomatoes and potatoes. Common food triggers are wheat, beef, eggs, coffee, milk, chocolate, colas and citrus. Take a sea salt and baking soda bath to detoxify and soothe your aches and pains. Add a few drops of lavender essential oil to help you relax and destress. Massage is also beneficial to help ease muscle tension that often accompanies pain syndromes.

ASTHMA
UNDERLYING EMOTION—FEELING STIFLED, SUPPRESSED AND FEELING LIKE CRYING

Asthma is on the rise with almost a 50 percent increase in the last decade. Emotional stress plays a large part in this disease along with food allergies, hypoglycemia, low thyroid, adrenal exhaustion and constipation.

If you suffer from asthma, it's important that you get the frequency and severity of your attacks under control. You must avoid dairy products because they generate mucus. You should avoid sulfites, MSG, caffeine, soft drinks and reduce your salt intake. Make your diet mostly vegetarian and focus on leafy-green, magnesium-rich vegetables. Magnesium helps to relax bronchial muscles.

You should know that cortisone drugs used to treat asthma eventually weaken your immune system, and drugstore over-the-counter remedies actually suppress symptoms and merely drive the congestion deeper into the body. The following natural supplements have been used for many years for asthma symptoms with positive results. Strengthen the adrenal glands with Core Level Adrenal and, if you're not allergic to bee products, Royal Jelly. For acute attacks, lobelia extract under the tongue is effective for chest muscle relaxation. Also, try a slice of raw onion under the tongue for 10–15 seconds to act as a bronchial dilator. Gingko biloba eases breathing. Echinacea and goldenseal extract will thin mucus. Take a magnesium gel cap of 400 milligrams at bedtime and antioxidants such as Carlson's ACES (vitamins A, C, E and selenium). Use quercetin, 1000 milligrams, and bromelain, 500 milligrams, as natural anti-inflammatories each day. Practice deep breathing to help bring asthmatic breathing under control.

CANDIDA
UNDERLYING EMOTION—UNTRUSTING, FRUSTRATION, ANGER

Candida is a stress-related condition marked by a seriously compromised immune response. *Candida albicans* normally lives harmlessly in our gastrointestinal tracts and genitourinary areas of our bodies. If our immune response is reduced, as mine was from repeated courses of antibiotics, a high-sugar diet and lack of rest and relaxation, candida then multiplies too quickly, causing major health problems. The yeast colonies establish a foothold and flourish throughout the body, releasing toxins into the bloodstream. To see if candida overgrowth could be contributing to your current state of health, take the following yeast screening developed by William Crook, MD.

CANDIDA AND YOUR HEALTH

Place a check in each box that describes you or a symptom you have experienced.

SECTION A—HISTORY

Scoring for Section A: At the end of each question is the score for a "yes" answer.

❑ Have you taken tetracycline or other antibiotics for acne for one month or longer? (35) ____

❑ Have you at any time in your life taken broad-spectrum antibiotics or other antibacterial medication for respiratory, urinary or other infections for two months or longer, or shorter courses four or more times in a one-year period? (35) ____

❑ Have you taken a broad-spectrum antibiotic drug even in a single dose? (6) ____

❑ Have you at any time in your life been bothered by persistent prostatitis, vaginitis or other problems affecting your reproductive organs? (25) ____

❑ Are you bothered by memory or concentration problems, and do you sometimes feel spaced out? (20) ____

❑ Do you feel sick all over, and in spite of visits to many physicians the causes haven't been found? (20) ____

❑ Have you been pregnant two or more times? (5) ____

❑ One time? (3) ____

❑ Have you taken birth control pills . . .

   ❑ For more than two years? (15) ____

   ❑ For six months to two years? (8) ____

❑ Have you taken steroids orally, by injection or by inhalation?

   ❑ For more than two weeks? (15) ____

   ❑ For two weeks or less? (6) ____

❑ Does exposure to perfumes, insecticides, fabric-shop odors and other chemicals provoke . . .

   ❑ Moderate to severe symptoms? (20) ____

   ❑ Mild symptoms? (5) ____

❑   Does tobacco smoke really bother you? (10)   _____

❑   Are your symptoms worse on damp, muggy days or in moldy places? (20)   _____

❑   Have you had athlete's foot, ringworm, jock itch or other chronic fungus infections of the skin or nails? (10)   _____

❑   Have such infections been severe or persistent? (20)   _____

  ❑ Mild to moderate? (10)   _____

  ❑ Do you crave sugar? (10)   _____

  Total Score Section A   _____

SECTION B—MAJOR SYMPTOMS

These symptoms are often present in persons with yeast-connected health challenges. Rate your response, using the following scoring system:

  3 points—Occasional or mild

  6 points—Frequent and/or moderately severe

  9 points—Severe and/or disabling

❑   Fatigue or lethargy?   _____

❑   Feeling of being drained?   _____

❑   Depression or manic depression?   _____

❑   Numbness, burning or tingling?   _____

❑   Headaches?   _____

❑   Muscle aches?   _____

❑   Muscle weakness or paralysis?   _____

❑   Pain and/or swelling in joints?   _____

❑   Abdominal pain?   _____

❑   Bloating, belching or intestinal gas?   _____

❑   Constipation and/or diarrhea?   _____

❑   Troublesome vaginal burning, itching or discharge?   _____

❑   Prostatitis?   _____

❑   Impotence?   _____

❑   Loss of sexual desire or feeling?   _____

❑   Endometriosis? _____

❑   Cramps and/or other menstrual irregularities? _____

❑   Premenstrual tension? _____

❑   Attacks of anxiety or crying? _____

❑   Cold hands or feet, low body temperature? _____

❑   Hypothyroidism? _____

❑   Shaking or irritable when hungry? _____

❑   Cystitis or interstitial cystitis? _____

Total Score Section B   _____

Section C—Additional yeast-related symptoms:

Scoring system for Section C:

> 1 point—Occasional or mild
>
> 2 points—Frequent or moderately severe
>
> 3 points—Severe and/or disabling

❑   Drowsiness, including inappropriate drowsiness? _____

❑   Irritability? _____

❑   Lack of coordination? _____

❑   Frequent mood swings? _____

❑   Insomnia? _____

❑   Dizziness or loss of balance? _____

❑   Pressure above ears or feeling of head swelling? _____

❑   Sinus problems or tenderness of cheekbones or forehead? _____

❑   Tendency to bruise easily? _____

❑   Eczema, itching eyes? _____

❑   Psoriasis? _____

❑   Chronic hives? _____

❑   Indigestion or heart burn? _____

❑   Sensitivity to milk, wheat, corn or other common foods? _____

❑   Mucus in stools? _____

❑   Rectal itching? _____

❏   Dry mouth or throat? _____

❏   Mouth rashes including white tongue? _____

❏   Bad breath? _____

❏   Foot, hair or body odor not relieved by washing? _____

❏   Nasal congestion or postnasal drip? _____

❏   Nasal itching? _____

❏   Sore throat? _____

❏   Laryngitis, loss of voice? _____

❏   Cough or recurrent bronchitis? _____

❏   Pain or tightness in chest? _____

❏   Wheezing or shortness of breath? _____

❏   Urinary frequency or urgency? _____

❏   Burning on urination? _____

❏   Spots in front of eyes or erratic vision? _____

❏   Burning or tearing eyes? _____

❏   Recurrent infections or fluid in ears? _____

❏   Ear pain or deafness? _____

Total Score Section C _____

Total Score Section A _____
Total Score Section B _____
Total Score Section C _____

GRAND TOTAL SCORE _____

How did you score?

Women with a score over 180 and men with a score over 140 almost certainly have yeast-connected health problems. Women with a score over 120 and men with a score over 90 probably have yeast-connected health problems. For scores in women over 60 and men over 40, yeast-connected health problems are possibly present. With scores less than 60 in women and less than 40 in men, yeast is less apt to be the cause of your health problems.

Most of the people whom I have worked with in my office have scored very high on the yeast questionnaire. And most of these people are the product of the antibiotic era.

The plan of attack at a glance is:

- Kill the yeast through diet change and supplement therapy.
- Avoid antibiotics unless absolutely necessary. There are natural antibiotic alternatives.
- Detoxify to cleanse the dead yeast from the body.
- Use enzyme therapy to strengthen the digestive system in order to assimilate nutrients. Strengthen the liver and kidneys. Replant healthy bowel flora with friendly bacteria.
- Rebuild immunity. Follow my *90-Day Immune System Makeover* (Siloam, 2000).

If you are battling any kind of digestive or intestinal problem, probiotics are a must. These gastrointestinal defenders are crucial in keeping your immune defenses in good working order. They consist mainly of lactobacillus acidophilus and lactobacillus bifidus, and they produce volatile fatty acids that provide metabolic energy. In addition, they help you digest food and amino acids, produce certain vitamins and, more importantly, make your lower intestine mildly acidic, which inhibits the growth of bad bacteria such as *E. coli,* which has caused serious illnesses in recent years.

Probiotic supplementation is absolutely essential in your fight against candida or any fungal infection because of the antifungal properties that these defenders possess. According to Dr. James F. Balch in his best-selling book *Prescription for Nutritional Healing* (Avery Publishing Group), the flora in a healthy colon should consist of at least 85 percent lactobacilli and 15 percent coliform bacteria. The typical colon bacteria count today is the reverse, which has resulted in gas, bloating, intestinal and systemic toxicity, constipation and malabsorption of nutrients, making it a perfect environment for the overgrowth of candida. By adding probiotics, that is lactobacillus acidophilus and lactobacillus bifidus supplements to your system, you will return your intestinal flora to a healthier balance and eliminate all of the problems of intestinal flora imbalance mentioned.

If you are on antibiotic therapy, it is vitally important that you supplement your digestive tract with probiotics or good bacteria because antibiotic use destroys your healthy bowel flora along with the harmful bacteria. Both L. acidophilus and L. bifidus promote proper digestion, help to normalize bowel function, prevent gas and candida overgrowth. This in turn keeps immunity high.

Store your probiotic formula in a cool, dry place. Some brands require refrigeration. I personally prefer and use Kyo-Dophilus from Wakunaga of America because it is milk-free and remains viable and stable even at high temperatures. It contains 1.5 billion live cells per capsule, is suitable for all ages and contains L. acidophilus, B. bifidum, and B. longum in a vegetable starch complex. In addition, it's free of preservatives, sugar, sodium, yeast, gluten, artificial colors and flavors and, as mentioned before, milk.

As a dietary supplement, take one capsule with a meal twice daily. Children under four should take a half capsule with a meal twice daily. If the child cannot swallow the capsule, simply open it and sprinkle in juice or on food.

This is a wonderful formula for optimally balanced intestinal health. Now let's turn our attention to a natural solution for antibiotics.

NATURAL ANTIBIOTICS

Right now you may be asking yourself, *If antibiotics can contribute to yeast overgrowth, then what can I use to treat infections that may arise after I've gone through the yeast eradication program?* You will be pleased to know that there are many natural substances that are powerful antibiotics from which to choose. The first one is biotic silver pure silver protein. It is a very powerful natural antibiotic and antifungal solution that is so strong and effective that it kills and removes from the body all bacteria, viruses and fungi within a short period of time. According to Gary Carlson, director of the Candida Wellness Center in Provo,

Utah, this natural antibiotic is extremely effective and overcomes serious infections. It has been approved by the Federal Drug Administration and is classified as a dietary mineral supplement. There are no side effects recorded in decades of use. Studies at the University of Toronto concluded that no toxicity, even in high dosages, results from using biotic silver.

Having sufficient pure silver protein in the body is like having a superior second immune system. Long ago when the earth was more fertile and our food supply was more pure and natural, there was more silver in the soil that would be absorbed into our food. In minute amounts, this silver would prevent infectious disease because no yeast, bacteria or virus can survive in the presence of silver. But today, due to the mining of silver for its monetary value and inorganic methods of farming, there is little silver left in the soil. In addition, strains of infectious organisms are so much stronger today that larger than normal amounts of silver are necessary to eradicate them.

Research indicates that biotic silver protein has been used successfully in the treatment against more than six hundred fifty diseases including allergies, athlete's foot, pneumonia, pleurisy, bladder infections, boils, candida yeast infections, cold sores, colds, flus, cystitis, dermatitis, fungal infection, indigestion, lupus, lyme disease, malaria, psoriasis, rhinitis, ring worm, sinus infections, staph, tonsillitis, viruses, warts and whooping cough.

I know you are probably excited about this wonderful product. However, you must know the difference between colloidal silver and biotic silver. Biotic silver is the most advanced form of colloidal silver for the therapeutic purpose of fighting infection available today. The superior effect comes from a special scientific process that allows it to reach negative microorganisms quickly and destroy them completely everywhere in the body. Once the pure silver protein has accomplished its goal, it is removed from the body with no toxic accumulation or side effects.

Silver particle size is important when it comes to a superior silver protein formula. In the case of biotic silver, it is certified to have silver particles down to .001 microns or smaller, which allows the particle to flow freely through even the smallest capillaries of the body and enter and be removed completely from the cells and tissues. It can even be given to infants and used during pregnancy.

Because it is a special proprietary formulation, it does no harm to human enzymes, hormones or any part of the body chemistry. For ordering information, see the references and product source section at the back of the book. Other choices include goldenseal, grapefruit seed concentrate, oil of oregano and olive leaf extract. These can be found in your local health food store.

Olive leaf is a 100 percent natural, herbal antibacterial, antiviral and antifungal extract taken from specific parts of the olive tree. In addition, it is a nontoxic immune system builder. Recently a more concentrated form of olive leaf extract has been developed and is marketed under the name *Defend*.

Goldenseal acts as an antibiotic and has anti-inflammatory and antibacterial properties. It's good for any infectious disease. If you use it at the first sign of cold, flu or sore throat, it may stop it from developing at all. If not, it will shorten the duration of the symptoms.

Oil of oregano is a very powerful antibacterial agent. Use it very sparingly.

Grapefruit seed extract is antifungal, antibacterial and antiviral. It is available in a liquid or capsule form. Nasal sprays are also available.

COLITIS
UNDERLYING EMOTION—FEAR, INSECURITY

The common causes of colitis are emotional stress, depression and anxiety, lack of fiber, food allergies, candida yeast involvement, vitamin K deficiency, too many antibiotics and excess sugar and refined foods in the diet.

Most colitis sufferers are between the ages of twenty and forty with stressful occupations or lifestyles. Natural therapies are very effective and can reduce the need for medications. Most cases are related to food allergies, which in turn cause an inflamed colon. Typically cheese, corn, wheat and eggs are the most common colitis triggers. Diet change is imperative in relieving and healing colitis. The following recommendations have been used with great success.

Dietary tips for overcoming colitis

- Clean up your diet.
- Avoid coffee, caffeine, nuts, dairy and citrus foods.
- Cut out sugar, wheat and spicy foods.
- Eat yogurt daily.
- Drink plenty of water daily, six to eight glasses. Make one glass a green drink.
- Make oatmeal, brown rice, steamed veggies, green salads and fresh fruits, especially apples, a part of your diet.
- Eat smaller meals to digest and assimilate your food easily.
- Practice relaxation techniques daily. Listen to soothing music.
- Take milk thistle extract for liver health.
- Have a cup of chamomile tea before bed sweetened with Stevia.
- Take BioK—probiotic culture liquid—for intestinal rebalancing and rebuilding.
- Calm the body with kava kava, valerian or passionflower before bed.
- For cramping, try cramp bark capsules.
- Take glucosamine sulfate, 500 milligrams daily, for mucous membrane rebuilding.
- Take Siberian ginseng to fortify the body during times of stress.
- Take Royal Jelly for adrenal gland health.

CONSTIPATION
UNDERLYING EMOTION—REFUSING TO RELEASE OLD TRAUMAS

The causes for constipation include insufficient amounts of fluid and fiber in the diet, and may also be a side effect of some drugs such as painkillers, antidepressants and iron tablets. Constipation also occurs during pregnancy.

Physical causes of stress are a major factor in constipation. A diet that contains too little fiber coupled with fast foods, fried foods, dairy foods, red meat, too much caffeine and alcohol all contribute to bowel irregularity. Consider a detoxification program to cleanse your system of stored wastes and toxins. I use Nature's Secret A.M./P.M. Ultimate Cleanse twice a year to insure that my system is as clean as possible.

Afterward, as a preventative take 400 milligrams of liquid magnesium gel caps daily. Take a probiotic bowel flora supplement such as BioK or Kyo-Dophilus. Take digestive enzymes from Enzymedica, Kyolic garlic liquid or capsules to normalize intestinal function and kill yeast. Have a green drink daily (Kyo- Green), and take flaxseed oil capsules.

You should avoid fats, sugars and fried foods along with dairy foods, as they hamper your body's efforts to rid itself of wastes. Remember, your body loves fiber. I call it *your body's little house cleaner.* It helps to sweep all of the toxins and wastes through your intestines in record time. There is a way to determine if you need to up your fiber intake. The following guidelines will insure that your elimination is optimal:

- There should be almost no gas or flatulence.
- The stool should be almost odorless, which means transit time is good.
- The stool should be light enough to float, indicating adequate fiber intake.
- The bowel movement should be effortless, daily and regular.

If you are not on track, simply add a fiber supplement until you achieve the desired results.

By using this guide, you will be able to make your constipation a thing of the past. Remember to drink plenty of water when adding fiber to the diet!

CYSTITIS
UNDERLYING EMOTION—ANGER, BLAMING OTHERS

Common causes include overuse of antibiotics, *E. coli* that migrates up the urethra, stress, kidney malfunction, food allergens, lack of water, poor elimination and a need for detoxification.

Cystitis is very common in women. As a matter of fact, bladder infections are the most frequent reason a woman seeks medical attention. You should begin treating this condition at the first sign of infection. Follow these steps:

- Follow my eating plan as outlined in part one. It is yeast-, sugar- and dairy-free.
- Drink six to eight glasses of unsweetened cranberry juice or take cranberry concentrate gel capsules as directed.
- Drink plenty of water.
- Eat watermelon or drink watermelon juice.
- Eliminate caffeine, chocolate, red meat, sugary foods, soft drinks and dairy foods.
- Take grapefruit seed extract capsules.
- Take Kyolic Garlic capsules daily if the problem is chronic.
- Take a liquid probiotic supplement like BioK daily.
- Have a green drink daily.

This protocol may also be used as a preventative maintenance program.

DEPRESSION
UNDERLYING EMOTION—ANGER, HOPELESSNESS

Causes include stress, nutritional deficiencies, nervous tension, poor diet, mononucleosis, thyroid disorders, allergies and serious physical disorders.

Depression is no exception when it comes to having a connection to brain depletion. When certain nutrients are not supplied to the brain, a negative set of emotions can occur and affect your ability to cope with stressful situations.

Depression has risen to epidemic proportions in this country.

More than 1.5 million people are being treated for it, and 30 million more can expect to suffer from it sometime in their lives. Women seem to be more susceptible to depression than men, perhaps because women are thought of as being more emotional, or it may be linked to a female reproductive hormone connection. At any rate, scientific studies reveal that by taking specific amino acids to restore the brain, depression can be alleviated.

Again, dangerous emotions play a part in this devastating condition that leads to depletion. The underlying origins for depression are bottled-up anger or aggression turned inward, great loss, the inability to express grief and negative emotional behavior often learned in childhood to control relationships. Drug-induced depression can also occur when prescription drugs create nutrient deficiencies. Amino acid deficiency also occurs during prolonged and intense stress, creating a biochemical imbalance with nutrient deficiencies.

DEPRESSION PROTOCOL

Nutrition is crucial and is the key to your brain's behavior. Eat foods that are rich in calcium, magnesium and B vitamins. Eat foods that contain tryptophan such as turkey, potatoes and bananas. Cut out sugary foods and caffeine and drink pure water only. Feed your brain a mixture of lecithin, wheat germ and brewer's yeast (take 2–3 tablespoons daily). You may sprinkle it on cereal or oatmeal. Follow my health-building eating plan.

The following natural supplements have been used with great success.

- *SAMe*–400 milligrams. This has been a blessing to depression sufferers, relieving both depression and pain in many instances.
- *Liquid serotonin*—Can be used when the serotonin level in the brain is depleted from depression and communication decreases. Serotonin is one of the neurotransmitters in the brain that helps us to feel calm and relaxed. Liquid serotonin can be used at any time of the day or night and by all ages.

It should be used in conjunction with other amino acids for optimal effectiveness.

- *Brain Link Complex*—A complete amino acid complex powder that creates neurotransmitter links for enhanced brain function. Brain Link was formulated by Billie J. Sahley, and I feel that it is the most complete neurotransmitter formula available today.
- CoQ_{10}—Stimulates immunity and helps decrease immuno-deficiency in times of chronic anxiety, depression and grief.
- *Carlson ACES*—Antioxidants are crucial when you are battling emotional illness.
- *Tyrosine*—Needed for brain function. This amino acid is excellent for people who have prolonged and intense stress. Uncontrollable stress may be prevented or reversed if tyrosine is taken either in capsule form or obtained in the diet. If you are taking a MAO inhibitor drug, you should not take tyrosine because it can raise your blood pressure.

EPSTEIN-BARR VIRUS (CHRONIC FATIGUE SYNDROME)
UNDERLYING EMOTION—INADEQUACY, INSECURITY, STRESS

The symptoms of this disorder include fatigue that does not resolve with bed rest, low-grade fever, throat infection, muscle weakness, gastrointestinal problems, sore lymph nodes, allergies, depression, loss of appetite and weight loss.

This is an illness that I have experienced and have overcome. This disease is also related to hypoadrenalism or adrenal exhaustion. In addition, there is a strong connection to *candida albicans* yeast infection. This is clearly a stress virus that attacks the body when it is at its lowest point. It is a complex syndrome with a wealth of causative factors. The typical chronic fatigue sufferer is female, usually between thirty and fifty years old, outgoing, productive, independent, active and an overachiever. This syndrome affects nearly two million people in America today. Considered medically incurable, it is increasing at an alarming rate. While it's true that no medical treatment or drug on the market today can help fatigue syndromes, and most hinder immune response and recovery, natural medicine offers hope and healing.

In addition to the following health-building suggestions, I recommend that you read my book *90-Day Immune System Makeover* (Siloam, 2000). It will give you the plan that I used to regain my health, and it will truly help you rebuild and rebalance your entire body. This is crucial if you are going to overcome this stubborn condition. It takes about four weeks to realize improvement, and three to six months or longer to feel normal again. Most people do respond to natural therapies in three to six months. Many people achieve near normal functioning in two years time even though the virus may persist in the body.

Again, it's important that you address the stress and emotional pain in your life. This virus has a strong emotional stress connection. The people who learn to identify and manage mental, emotional and physical stress in their lives recover the quickest. Laughter is truly the best medicine.

The following guidelines will also help your recovery.

1. First, you must strengthen your nervous system. I recommend a B-complex supplement, SAMe, boosting serotonin levels or taking liquid serotonin and gingko biloba.
2. Boost your liver health with milk thistle seed extract and dandelion tea sweetened with Stevia. Apply warm castor oil packs to the liver area three times weekly.

BALANCING YOUR BODY CHEMISTRY

For hormone balance, use Dr. Janet's Balanced by Nature Progesterone Cream (information in the back of the book). Also take fifteen to twenty drops in water daily of any of the following extracts:

- Suma
- Reishi mushroom
- Maitake mushroom
- Siberian ginseng
- Enzyme therapy, important for digestion, inflammation and energy

- Purify from Enzymedica
- CoQ$_{10}$, 60 milligrams, four times daily
- BioK (acidophilus cultures)
- Bromelain, 1000 milligrams daily, divided between meals
- Body energizers
- Carnitine, 2000 milligrams daily
- Core Level Adrenal Gland supplement
- Antiviral, antibacterial, antifungal (choose one or more)
  Grapefruit seed extract
  Biotic silver
  Olive leaf extract
  St. John's wort (antiviral and also an antidepressant)
  Oil of oregano

SPECIAL CONSIDERATIONS

- Aspirin, NSAIDS or cortisone can hamper your body's ability to maintain bone strength and adrenal health.
- Avoid tobacco in all forms because it is an immunity destroyer.
- Have a protein shake each morning. This is crucial for rebuilding the body.
- Have a green drink (Kyo-Green from Wakunaga) for healthy blood chemistry.
- Symptoms are reduced by aerobic exercise. Begin with a short walk each day.
- Keep your bowel function optimal by adding fiber to your diet.
- Drink plenty of water, eight to ten glasses per day. This is especially important when increasing your fiber intake.
- Follow the eating plan as outlined in part one of this book.
- Limit sugar, caffeine and alcohol.
- Use Stevia extract as a natural sweetener.
- Be patient with yourself. Recovery takes time. Be good to yourself; you deserve it!

FIBROMYALGIA
UNDERLYING EMOTION—RESENTMENT OR FEELING UNLOVED

The causes of this disease are a compromised immune system often preceded by a stressful event, magnesium deficiency or possible viral connection. Fibromyalgia is commonly associated with mitral valve prolapse.

Up to ten million Americans, mostly women, suffer from fibromyalgia. It's considered to be a stress-related immune disorder with the central cause being a low level of serotonin and reduced-growth hormone. It is best described as an arthritic/muscle disease.

Common symptoms include painful, tender, recurrent points aching all over the body, diffuse musculo-skeletal pain and stiffness, fatigue, weakness, headaches, confusion, migraines, chronic bowel problems, poor sleep, nervous symptoms, hypoglycemia, shortness of breath, cardiovascular problems and allergies.

Fibromyalgia may be greatly improved by the following natural therapies.

1. Follow my eating plan. (Avoid sugars, fats, red meat and caffeine.)
2. Take Kyolic garlic by Wakunaga daily.
3. Have a green drink daily.
4. Use Royal Jelly.
5. To reduce pain and inflammation try:
   a. Dr. Janet's Balanced by Nature Glucosamine Cream
   b. Quercetin, 1,000 milligrams
   c. Bromelain, 1,500 milligrams
6. For brain balance try:
   a. Brain Link (amino acid powder)
   b. Gingko biloba
   c. GABA
7. To assist the musculo-skeletal system, try:
   a. L-carnitine, 1,000 milligrams
   b. Magnesium gel caps and malic acid
   c. B-complex

8. Natural antidepressants to raise serotonin levels:
   a. SAMe, 800 milligrams daily
   b. St. John's wort, 300 milligrams daily
9. For restful sleep:
   a. Valerian root extract
   b. Kava kava
   c. Passionflower
10. To boost immunity:
    a. Vitamin C, 3,000 milligrams daily
    b. CoQ_{10}, 60 milligrams three times daily
    c. Have a regular monthly massage.
    d. Listen to your relaxation tape that you have recorded.
    e. Take the stress-relieving bath as outlined.
    d. Develop your prayer life.

HEARTBURN
UNDERLYING EMOTION—FEAR

The causes of heartburn can include excessive consumption of spicy or fatty and fried foods, alcohol, coffee, citrus fruits, chocolate, hiatal hernia, ulcers, gallbladder problems, allergies and enzyme deficiency.

If you live with chronic heartburn and indigestion, chances are you are aging faster than you should. When you have heartburn your body's energy is reduced, toxins accumulate, allergic reactions occur and your immune defenses get low. What's more, as you get older your digestion weakens because you produce less stomach acid.

Without enough stomach acid or HCl, we cannot digest proteins well. This will lead to amino acid deficiency. In addition, the following causes also contribute to this uncomfortable condition—yeast overgrowth from antibiotic therapy, too much caffeine, alcohol, sugar, wheat or dairy allergies, overeating and poor food combining, especially eating fruit with or after meals.

First and foremost you will need to supplement your digestive system with digestive enzymes from a plant source. Choose the one from Enzymedica that fits your profile.

184

Have a green drink daily, and take a probiotic supplement each day such as BioK or Kyo-Dophilus. To soothe the burn, take Enzymatic Therapy DGL tablets until your system balances. Try not to eat when you are stressed or upset, as this only makes digestion more difficult. Have a cup of peppermint or mint medley tea from Celestial Seasonings to help complete digestion before you go to bed. As your digestion normalizes, you will have more energy, sleep better and feel lighter and more energetic.

When it comes to supplemental enzymes, there are two sources— plant and animal. I use plant enzymes personally because animal enzymes, commonly known as pancreatic enzymes, are from the pancreas of slaughter-house animals. You need to ask yourself, *Am I going to risk supplementing my body with enzymes taken from the pancreas of an animal that may have been in poor health, had cancer or any other disease?* In addition, animal enzymes are not as digestively active as plant enzymes.

Plant enzymes work throughout the entire digestive system and in the blood. Not all enzyme products are alike or equal in their activity in the body. You must look for the appropriate codes approved by the FDA to insure active enzyme activity. Another thing to watch for is fillers such as leftover fibers and cellulose added to the formula.

Look for an enzyme supplier that uses a standard system for ensuring the potency of their enzymes. The system for determining enzyme potency used by the American food industry is derived from the Food and Chemical Code, or FCC. Find an enzyme supplier that measures and reports the enzyme product levels in FCC units. This way you will be assured of active, potent enzyme activity.

I have found a wonderful company by the name of Enzymedica, located in Punta Gorda, Florida, that manufactures a superior line of enzymes that I use exclusively in my practice. They meet all the criteria for activity and potency. Furthermore, they have formulas specifically tailored to the four deficiency syndromes. You may be wondering at this point as to how and when you should take your oral plant enzymes. In order for the plant enzymes to provide all the benefits during the digestion process, they need to be taken when their activity will be compatible with what is occurring during digestion. I instruct my clients to take their enzymes at the beginning of a meal because they give higher effectiveness in digesting food. Enzymes could be taken at the end of the meal, but the rate of efficiency will not be as good due to the fact that acidity has been built up during the digestive process, thereby, lessening some of the enzymes effects that have low pHs. According to "The White Paper" by Dr. M. Mamadou, who is a microbiologist and enzymologist, for complete assimilation it is recommended that oral enzymes be taken at the beginning of the meal, halfway during the meal and at the end of the meal.

Plant enzymes help to develop and maintain a proper digestive system and can be used in varying formulas to treat certain ailments. Enzymes from a plant source are superior to an animal source because plant enzymes become active as soon as they enter their body. These enzymes are a blessing to us in our modern times when over the years, we have used up so much of our own enzyme potential, thus making enzymes extremely necessary to efficiently digest.

ENZYMES AND DIGESTION

Enzymes are crucial for improved immune function. This is because they turn foods that we eat into energy and unlock this energy for the body's use. Our bodies make two basic types of enzymes—digestive and metabolic. The strength of our enzyme activity is important in building a stronger immune system as well as healthier blood.

Our bodies secrete digestive enzymes to help us break down food into nutrients and wastes. Our digestive enzymes include pepsin, lipase, protease, amylase, trypsin and ptyalin.

We also receive enzymes from raw foods that we eat and by taking enzyme supplements. I strongly recommend that you supplement your body with enzymes. This is plain old common sense.

In our busy lifestyles and hectic schedules, we overcook, microwave and overprocess our foods, killing all or most of the enzymes. While it's true that we occasionally eat raw foods that do contain live enzyme activity, our consumption of cooked dead enzyme foods is greater. Unless we supplement, this leaves our bodies a big job of producing more enzymes to break down these cooked foods.

I have seen people gain more energy, lose weight, sleep better and feel better in general after supplementing their bodies with enzymes. This is because our bodies work more efficiently with proper enzyme activity. No excess energy has to be expended by the body on the process of digestion. It has been said that we are only as healthy as what we assimilate and eliminate. After awhile you will assimilate or digest better with the help of supplemental enzymes and eliminate better by detoxifying your body.

A variety of supplemental enzymes are available through different sources. It's very important that you use an enzyme supplement tailored to your particular situation. Also, make sure that the doses you take are measured in active units, which are the most potent.

In my research, I found that there are four basic types of enzyme deficiencies. A lack of protease limits your ability to digest proteins. A lack of lipase hampers your ability to digest fats. A deficiency of amylase affects your ability to digest carbohydrates. A deficiency of any two or all three enzymes can lower the quality of your life because of lowered immune response.

Enzymes have far-reaching benefits. They deliver nutrients, carry away toxic wastes, digest food, purify the blood, deliver hormones by feeding and fortifying the endocrine system, balance cholesterol and triglyceride levels, feed the brain and cause no harm to the body. All of these contribute to the strengthening of the immune system.

There are many additional benefits to therapeutic enzyme therapy as well. If we fortify the endocrine system, get the bowels working regularly and digest our food with the help of enzymes instead of turning it to fat, then we can be truly successful at losing weight and gaining energy.

Younger-looking skin is another benefit of proper enzyme

supplementation. Enzymes fight the aging process by increasing the blood supply to the skin, delivering life-giving nutrients and then carrying away waste products that can make your skin look old, tired and wrinkled. Because circulation slows down as we age, enzyme supplementation becomes crucial as we grow older. Enzymes are important in keeping your immune system in good condition and functioning optimally. The next question is, What type of enzymes do you need to digest food? By enzyme supplementation we will help the body complete the digestive process without overstressing the body's enzyme making potential. We will then be in a much more favorable position to fight biological and system malfunctions while boosting our immune systems to a higher level.

I have found the following four formulas by Enzymedica to be extremely effective personally and in clinical use.

The first formula is called *Digest*. This formula speeds digestion of food while reducing the body's need to produce digestive enzymes. Take one capsule with each meal. One capsule is usually sufficient for alleviating poor digestion. If you are in poor health, you may need two to five capsules until your digestion improves.

Digest contains high-potency multiple enzymes along with lactobacillus acidophilus to help maintain healthy bowel flora. This formula helps you to digest protein, starch, fat, sugar and fiber.

The next formula is *Purify*. It contains the highest available potency of protease to help digest protein invaders in the blood. This would include parasites, fungal, bacteria and viruses, which are covered by a protein film. The enzyme protease breaks down the undigested protein, toxins and debris in the blood, thereby unburdening the immune system so it can concentrate its full action.

The recommended dosage is three capsules first thing in the morning and right before bed. This formula is excellent for candida sufferers who traditionally have difficulty with protein digestion and tend to have a toxic load in their bloodstream.

Next on the list is *Lypo*. This is an excellent formula that contains the highest available potency of lipase, which digests fats in the blood and digestive tract. This will help to lower cholesterol and triglycerides. It provides additional support for carbohydrates and dairy products and aids elimination.

The recommended dosage is two capsules with each meal. If you are overweight, meaning more than twelve pounds over your ideal weight, the dosage is three capsules with meals. According to research, people who are obese are usually low in lipase.

Gastro is the last formula on the list of super enzymes. This formula helps to soothe the gastrointestinal system and alleviate abdominal discomfort. This formula helps to relieve the burning and irritation that some people experience with digestion.

You can see that enzymes can greatly improve your life. DicQue Fuller, PhD, DSc, author of *The Healing Power of Enzymes,* said, "Anytime we suffer from an acute or chronic illness, it is almost certain an enzyme depletion exists!" I highly recommend that you add her book to your library if you want to learn more about enzymes. I call them God's sparks of life.

Look at your own symptoms and characteristics in the following chart to determine which enzymes you may need to start adding to your program.

DETERMINING YOUR ENZYME NEEDS

Place a check mark in each box that describes a symptom you have experienced.

AMYLASE DEFICIENCY

❏ Hypoglycemia	❏ Breaking out of the skin, rash
❏ Depression	❏ Mood swings
❏ Allergies	❏ PMS
❏ Hot flashes	❏ Fatigue
❏ Cold hands and feet	❏ Neck and shoulder aches
❏ Sprue	❏ Inflammation

PROTEASE DEFICIENCY

❏ Back weakness	❏ Fungal forms
❏ Constipation	❏ High blood pressure
❏ Insomnia	❏ Hearing problems
❏ Parasites	❏ Gum disorders
❏ Gingivitis	

LIPASE DEFICIENCY

- ❏ Aching feet, arthritis
- ❏ Cystitis
- ❏ Gallbladder stress
- ❏ Hay fever
- ❏ Psoriasis
- ❏ Constipation
- ❏ Heart problems
- ❏ Bladder problems
- ❏ Acne
- ❏ Gall stones
- ❏ Prostate problems
- ❏ Urinary weakness
- ❏ Diarrhea

COMBINATION DEFICIENCY

- ❏ Chronic allergies
- ❏ Diverticulitis
- ❏ Chronic fatigue
- ❏ Immune depressed conditions
- ❏ Common colds
- ❏ Irritable bowel
- ❏ Sinus infection

Once you determine your particular enzyme deficiency, you may then choose the Enzymedica plant enzyme formula that bests suits your profile.

HEART DISEASE

Heart disease claims the lives of over 720,000 people each year. It is the number one killer of Americans. The following risk factors are associated with increased heart disease.

- Male or postmenopausal women
- Age
- History of heart disease in the family
- High blood cholesterol
- Smoking
- Obesity
- Lack of exercise
- Stress
- High blood pressure

Some of these risk factors are beyond your control while others are within your control. Luckily, the most dangerous risk factors are the ones that you can do something about. They are smoking, high blood pressure and high cholesterol. If you decide to take a statin drug to lower your cholesterol, keep in mind that any of the statins also lower the CoEnzyme Q_{10} level in your body and may cause liver damage.

I recommend that you supplement your body with CoQ_{10} whether you are on medication or not for cholesterol problems. CoQ_{10} actually helps prevent heart attacks, boosts immunity, lowers blood pressure, is a powerful antioxidant and even relieves periodontal disease according to some studies.

Supplement with the following to keep your cardiovascular system healthy.

1. *Taurine*—1,000 milligrams twice daily. Taurine helps to balance the calcium and potassium in the heart as well as increasing the function of the left ventricle without changing the blood pressure.

2. *Carnitine*—1,000 to 3,000 milligrams per day in divided doses for high cholesterol and high triglycerides. Many people ask me how to raise the HDL or "good cholesterol" levels. I have found that carnitine in the right doses can help to accomplish a desirable HDL level.

3. *Chromium picolinate*—200 micrograms per day, 400 micrograms if you weigh more than 150 pounds. Chromium helps to lower triglycerides and cholesterol while raising HDL levels.

4. *Magnesium*—Most people with coronary artery disease or CAD are deficient in magnesium. Magnesium is crucial to a healthy heart, and it acts as a muscle relaxant.

5. *Vitamin E*—Vitamin E is a very important antioxidant. When vitamin E is taken daily, studies have shown a lower risk of fatal heart attacks.

6. CoQ_{10}—The recommended dose is 100 milligrams per day if you have CAD or high blood pressure. If you suffer from congestive heart failure, the dose is 300 to 500 milligrams per day.

7. *Anxiety Control*—As directed on the bottle as needed for anxiety or stress.

8. *Ester C*–2,000 to 5,000 milligrams per day in divided doses.
9. *Hawthorn berry*–As directed on product label. Hawthorn helps to improve circulation of the blood to the heart by dilating blood vessels and relieving arterial spasms.
10. *Kyo-Green*–Have a green drink daily for healthy blood chemistry.
11. *Garlic or aspirin therapy*–Taken each day, garlic is an alternative to aspirin and is at least as potent. Both thin the blood, thereby discouraging clots that can block arteries.

HEMORRHOIDS
UNDERLYING EMOTION—FEAR, ANGER, FEELING BURDENED

The physical causes for hemorrhoids include constipation, pregnancy, lack of exercise, too much sitting, liver exhaustion, allergies, obesity, not enough water and too much junk food.

Many Americans suffer from this painful, common condition. Most of the time constipation plays a large part in the development of hemorrhoids. This being the case, follow the guidelines for constipation in addition to the recommendations listed here. To relieve inflammation and promote healing: Ester C, 300 milligrams daily; magnesium gel caps, 400 milligrams at bedtime as a stool softener and muscle relaxant; Carlson's ACES; avoid caffeine, sugar and low-fiber refined foods. Eat small meals and take 1 tablespoon of olive or flax seed oil before each meal.

Use Hemorrhoid Relief from Bioforce Homeopathic remedies. Take a brisk thirty-minute walk daily to promote healthy circulation. Use ice packs and witch hazel to help to cool the pain and inflammation until improvement occurs.

INSOMNIA
UNDERLYING EMOTIONAL CONNECTION—FEAR, GUILT

Physical causes include stress, asthma, hypoglycemia, indigestion, pain, drugs and muscle aches.

The causes of insomnia are varied. Anxiety, depression, tension and chronic stress are the most common psychological factors. Pain is another cause for insomnia. If you consume coffee, iced tea or soft drinks that contain sugar and caffeine, you should know that these drinks all contribute to sleepless nights. Sleep disorders such as snoring or sleep apnea can be serious as they are often linked to irregular heartbeat, high blood pressure and decreased work productivity due to excessive fatigue.

Insomnia can be a particularly troublesome condition because the more you try to fall asleep, the more you cannot. Commercial sleeping pills are not the answer, although they are highly popular these days. They can interfere with your ability to dream.

Dreaming is your mind's way of getting rid of stored stress. To suppress this natural way to resolve stress is counterproductive. In addition, sleep aids can be habit forming.

The following protocol has been used to naturally deal with insomnia. Remember to address any guilt or fear that you may be experiencing or that you may have buried deep inside. Use the scripture verses to help and reassure you.

Before bed take a warm Epsom salts bath with lavender oil added. This will relax your muscles and mind, promoting restful sleep. Try some Sleepy Time tea or chamomile tea sweetened with Stevia extract. CalMax Powder, which is a highly absorbable calcium-magnesium powder, will help you sleep through the night. Kava kava and passionflower are natural relaxers along with valerian root to help ease tension and cause you to feel sleepy.

Carbohydrates can help to induce sleep. Pasta for dinner with vegetables and no meat is the way to go. You may also snack on brown rice, bananas or warm milk with honey. But do not eat late at night. Make your last meal of the day a light one.

You may try 0.3 milligrams of melatonin on a temporary basis to help reset your biological clock. Consider exercise. It is a wonderful stress reliever, which will in turn lighten your mental load. This can allow sleep to occur naturally without medication.

KIDNEY PROBLEMS (STONES, INFECTIONS)
UNDERLYING EMOTIONS—UNRESOLVED ANGER, CRITICISM, FAILURE, SHAME

Common physical causes are excess sugar, red meat, carbonated drinks, caffeine in the diet, diabetes, allergies, heavy metal poisoning, excess aluminum, EFA deficiency, overuse of prescription drugs, B vitamin and magnesium deficiency and overuse of aspirin and salt and diuretics.

Kidney problems can be prevented through improved diet and herb and supplement therapy. Have a green drink (Kyo-Green or liquid chlorophyll) every morning. Follow with a low-salt, low-protein, vegetarian diet for at least one month. Avoid all refined, fried and fatty foods and soft drinks during the healing phase. Eliminate dairy and animal protein.

To reduce kidney inflammation, try quercetin, 1,000 milligrams daily; Bromelain, 1,500 milligrams daily; B complex with B_6; magnesium, 800 milligrams daily; flax oil; choline/inositol capsules daily.

To help reverse kidney damage, use gingko biloba, Enzymedica Purify capsules and one spirulina capsule daily.

For infection, try cranberry capsules as directed on the bottle and biotic silver echinacea extract as directed on the bottle.

General rules for improved kidney function

- Drink eight glasses of pure water each day.
- Avoid NSAIDS (Advil, Motrin, Aleve), which have been associated with impaired kidney function.
- Avoid smoking and second-hand smoke.
- Take a brisk walk every day.
- Apply castor oil packs to kidney area alternating with ginger packs to stimulate circulation and flow. (Instructions for castor oil packs can be found at health food stores.)
- Do not use antacids (Tums, etc.) for indigestion because they may increase the risk of kidney stones.

LIVER PROBLEMS

UNDERLYING EMOTION—ANGER, FRUSTRATION

Symptoms of liver damage include poor digestion, fatigue, weight gain, sluggish system, depression, food and chemical sensitivities, constipation, nausea, dizziness, jaundiced skin, skin itching and congestion.

A healthy liver is truly vital to a healthy, robust life. This is because the health and vitality of every body system depend on the vitality of your liver. There are many common causes of liver dysfunction, including consuming too much alcohol or drugs, too much sugar, eating too many refined foods and preservatives, too much animal protein or not consuming enough fiber, exposure to toxic chemical and pollutants, stress, candida and chronic sinus infection.

Fortunately, the liver has amazing regenerative powers. It will take six months to a year to regenerate the liver and improve its function. The following recommendations have shown results time and time again.

LIVER SUPPORT

- Exercise daily—your liver is dependent on high-quality oxygen coming into the lungs.
- Drink pure water with lemon each day, eight to ten glasses.
- Keep fats low in your diet.
- Detoxify your body.
- Avoid acid-forming foods (red meat, caffeine, alcohol, dairy products and fried foods).
- Increase potassium-rich foods such as seafood and dried fruits.
- Increase chlorophyll-rich foods like leafy greens, or have a green drink daily.
- Increase sulfur-rich foods like eggs, garlic and onions.

TO ENHANCE LIVER FUNCTION

- Milk thistle seed liquid extract
- Dandelion root extract

- Artichoke capsules
- Reishi or maitake mushroom extract
- Royal Jelly
- Germanium, 150 milligrams
- BioK—acidophilus liquid cultures
- Antioxidants—CoQ_{10}, 100 milligrams daily; beta carotene, 10,000 international units; vitamin C (Ester C), 3,000 milligrams daily
- Optimal bowel function (two to three bowel movements daily)

LUPUS
UNDERLYING EMOTION—HOPELESSNESS, GIVING UP

Causes include viral infections, too many antibiotics or prescription drugs, allergies, emotional stress, reaction to certain chemicals, overgrowth of candida yeast and chronic fatigue syndrome.

Lupus is a multisystem, autoimmune, inflammatory, viral disease that affects over half a million Americans. Most sufferers are black or Hispanic women. This devastating disease occurs when the immune system becomes disoriented and creates antibodies that attack its own connective tissue. Joints and connective tissue are affected, causing arthritis-like symptoms. The kidneys and lymph nodes become inflamed along with the heart, brain and central nervous system. The immune system must be addressed and toxins must be neutralized before improvement occurs.

The following suggestions have been successful in keeping lupus under control and manageable.

1. Take a walk every day to relieve stress and for exercise.
2. Rest and sleep enough each day.
3. Focus on your prayer life.
4. Food therapy—eat fresh foods, avoid the nightshade vegetables that may aggravate lupus—tobacco, tomatoes, eggplant and peppers.

196

5. Have a potassium drink daily. Use this recipe to create your drink:

   Juice in a juicer: 3 carrots, 3 stalks celery, ½ bunch spinach, 1 Tbsp. snipped parsley, 1 tsp. Bragg's Liquid Aminos. Makes one 12-oz. glass.

6. Follow my recommended eating plan.
7. Have a green drink daily.
8. To reduce inflammation take:

   a. Quercetin, 1,000 milligrams
   b. Bromelain, 1,500 milligrams
   c. MSM capsules, 800 milligrams daily

9. For arthritis symptoms take:

   a. Glucosamine, 1,500 milligrams
   b. Germanium, 150 milligrams
   c. L-carnitine, 1,000 milligrams

10. For stress relief choose one or more:

    a. Siberian ginseng extract
    b. Reishi mushroom extract
    c. GABA
    d. SAMe, 800 milligrams daily
    e. Core Level Adrenal
    f. Kava kava extract

11. For muscle pain take:

    a. Magnesium gel capsules, 400 milligrams twice daily
    b. Malic acid
    c. B-complex vitamins

12. To boost immunity take:

    a. Astragalus extract
    b. Royal Jelly
    c. Vitamin C, 3,000 milligrams daily

13. For hormone balance: Dr. Janet's Balanced by Nature Progesterone Cream

PAIN
UNDERLYING EMOTION—GUILT, PUNISHMENT

Common symptoms include sharp, shooting twinges or a dull ache, numbness, muscle wasting and poor reflexes.

The physical causes of pain include adrenal and pituitary exhaustion, obesity, internal or external tumors, poor nutrition, overly acidic diet and poor muscle development.

Emotional and mental stress can eventually manifest as physical pain. Pain is almost individual and signals us to attend to its underlying cause. Pain dampens your strength and spirit, causing depression. While painkillers allow you to temporarily ignore the pain so you can work, live and function better, they do nothing to address the cause of the pain. In addition, pain relievers can be addictive or damaging to the stomach lining as well as the liver and kidneys. There are natural methods to overcome pain in the body. They work at a very deep level in the body, relaxing, soothing and calming the area in pain. The following recommendations have been proven to aid in the relief of many different pain syndromes.

- Avoid caffeine, sugar and salty foods that create an over-acidic system.
- Have a green drink each day.
- Eat a vegetarian diet, low in fats and high in minerals.
- Consider chiropractic adjustments, massage therapy and therapeutic baths.
- Consider magnet therapy.

Herbal pain relievers

- White willow bark—anti-inflammatory and analgesic
- Kava kava—relieves stress from chronic pain or injury
- Valerian—a sedative that will help you relax and sleep
- St. John's wort—for nerve damage and to lift the spirits

Use enzymes to reduce inflammation

- Enzymedica's Purify
- Bromelain

- Quercetin
- MSM
- Boswellia

PAINKILLERS FROM NATURE

- DLPA, 1,000 milligrams daily
- GABA, 750 milligrams
- Glucosamine caps and Dr. Janet's Balanced by Nature Glucosamine Cream
- Magnesium, 800 milligrams at bedtime

SINUS PROBLEMS
UNDERLYING EMOTION—IRRITATION

Would you believe that one in three Americans suffers from a chronic sinus infection? Given the emotional connection, it is possible that one in three Americans is also irritated. That is certainly something to think about. Consider all the road rage, short tempers and irrational behavior in this country. With one in three Americans being irritated, it begins to make sense.

Other physical causes of sinus problems are allergies, too much dairy food, too much sugar, salt and fried foods, poor food combining, constipation, poor circulation and a bacterial, fungal or viral infection.

This is a very uncomfortable condition because the sufferer feels worn out, tired, has headaches, runny nose and inflamed nasal passages with postnasal drip, which makes it especially hard to sleep. There may be nausea and indigestion from swallowed mucus, eye pain, tooth pain and loss of taste and smell. Follow my eating plan and add the following recommendations:

- To address the infection—Biotic silver or grapefruit seed extract capsules and nasal spray, olive leaf extract capsules
- For congestion—Breathe Easy tea from Traditional Medicinals; Ester C, 3,000 milligrams daily; echinacea extract, 15 drops in water four times daily

199

- To boost immunity—astragalus capsules, B complex with pantothenic acid, Kyolic garlic capsules as directed

Keep in mind that over-the-counter drugstore sinus medications only suppress symptoms and may drive the infection deeper into the sinus cavities. Natural medicine goes to the root cause.

THYROID HEALTH AND THE IMMUNE SYSTEM
UNDERLYING EMOTION—HOPELESS, STIFLED

Your thyroid gland is the thermostat of your body. It produces hormones to help keep your metabolic rate stable and to keep energy-producing and energy-using processes in balance. If it is depleted or deficient, the rest of the body will function improperly, leading to lower immunity. Thyroid problems can cause many recurring illnesses and fatigue.

To test yourself for an underactive thyroid, take this self test developed by Broda Barnes.[3] Keep a basal thermometer by your bedside. Before retiring, shake down the thermometer and place it within easy reach of your bed. In the morning before arising, lie still and place it under your armpit for ten minutes. Keep quiet and still! Any motion can upset the reading. Do this for seven to ten days consecutively.

DAILY THYROID MONITORING

	DATE	TEMPERATURE
1.	_____	_____
2.	_____	_____
3.	_____	_____
4.	_____	_____
5.	_____	_____
6.	_____	_____
7.	_____	_____
8.	_____	_____
9.	_____	_____
10.	_____	_____

Women should not take a reading during the first few days of their menstrual cycle or at the middle day of their cycle because body temperature fluctuates during these times. A normal reading is between 97.8 and 98.2. A temperature below 97.6 degrees Fahrenheit may indicate low-thyroid function. Record your readings for the next ten days. If your temperature is consistently below 97.6, you should add the following supplements to your emotional makeover program.

SUPPLEMENTS

- Kelp—contains iodine
- Raw Thyroid Glandular—helps to replace deficient thyroid hormone
- B-complex vitamin—helps improve thyroid function and immune function
- Essential fatty acids—necessary for proper thyroid gland function
- Or see your physician for Armor Thyroid, available by prescription only.

HYPOTHYROIDISM

The cause of hypothyroidism is the underproduction of the thyroid hormone.

This condition currently affects over five million Americans. Women make up the largest percentage of sufferers, usually between the ages of thirty to fifty. Symptoms of the often underdiagnosed disease are as follows—profound fatigue, weight gain with slow metabolism, depression, cold hands and feet, constipation, hair thinning or loss and enlarged thyroid gland. If you can relate to any of these symptoms, have a simple blood test performed to check your TSH, T_3 and T_4 levels.

If you are not currently on thyroid medication or if your condition is mild, you may use the following natural supplements to increase thyroid function:

- Kelp tablets as a natural source of iodine (as directed on the bottle)

- Core Level Thyroid from Nutri-West of Florida
- Antioxidants to protect the thyroid gland
- CoQ_{10}, 100 milligrams daily, and Carlson ACES

For memory improvement, use Wakunaga's Neurologic. To enhance thyroid function especially during perimenopause and menopause, use Dr. Janet's Balanced by Nature Progesterone Cream as directed.

Avoid the following foods that suppress thyroid function—peanuts, mustard, millet, soy and cabbage. These foods prevent iodine use in the body. Iodine-rich foods are excellent for thyroid function. They include mushrooms, garlic and onions. Make sure you use salt or herb-salt that contains iodine. Take a thirty-minute walk to stimulate your metabolism.

VICTORY

That takes us to the end of our list. If you've seen yourself and your symptoms in any of these sections, please don't be alarmed. Start your new beginning by making a few promises to yourself right now.

PROMISE YOURSELF

To be so strong that nothing can disturb your peace of mind.

To talk health, happiness and prosperity to every person you meet.

To make all your friends feel that there is something in them.

To look at the sunny side of everything and make your optimism come true.

To think only of the best, to work only for the best and expect only the best.

To be just as enthusiastic about the success of others as you are about your own.

To forget the mistakes of the past and press on to the greater achievements of the future.

To wear a cheerful countenance at all times and give every living creature you meet a smile.

202

To give so much time to improvement of yourself that you
    have no time to criticize others.
To be too large for worry, too noble for anger, too strong for
    fear and too happy to permit the presence of trouble.

—AUTHOR UNKNOWN

EPILOGUE

Now we come to the end of dangerous emotions. It is my sincere prayer that this book has helped you to determine how emotions can impact the quality of your life. Sometimes the initial traumatic splash happens in childhood from divorce, abuse, abandonment and lack of approval. Or it may be that your life has always been good until lately. Maybe you have personally experienced divorce, the death of a loved one, family problems or financial ruin. Whatever the case, if you do not replenish, renew and rebuild yourself emotionally, physically and spiritually, then you may eventually suffer a setback in your emotional and/or physical self.

This book is written from my heart to yours. It is a wake-up call to alert you in just the right time so that you will not be an emotional statistic but a victorious survivor who has been strengthened by adversity and trials. You have become wiser for it. You have learned that while stress and emotions are a part of life, it is how you *act*, rather than *react*, that is key to overcoming dangerous emotions.

Now, go forth. Put on the whole armor of God. Love, forgive, trust and live!

Blessed is the man who perseveres under trial, because when he has stood the test, he will receive the crown of life that God has promised to those who love him.

—JAMES 1:12

NOTES

CHAPTER 1
START WHERE YOU ARE

1. The material included in "The Stress Level" was reprinted by permission of the Midwest Center for Stress and Anxiety, 106 N. Church St., P. O. Box 205, Oak Harbor, OH 43449. Phone: (800) 944-9460. Fax: (419) 898-0669.

2. Hara Estroff Marano, "Children of Divorce Twenty-Five Years Later," *USA Weekend* (September 15–17, 2000): 16–17.

3. Lucinda Bassett, Attacking Anxiety, Stress and Depression, in cooperation with The Midwest Center for Stress and Anxiety. This program includes sixteen audio cassette sessions, a fifteen-chapter study guide and a corresponding set of quick reference cards. To order by toll-free telephone, call (800) 586-4014. To order online, go to www.AnxietySolution.com.

CHAPTER 2
ADD THE MISSING PIECES

1. Billie J. Sahley, Ph.D., *GABA: The Anxiety Amino Acid* (San Antonio, TX: Pain & Stress Publications, 1998).

2. Ibid.

3. Leo Galland, M.D., "When stress shatters, magnesium saves," *Great Life* (October 1998): 36–37.

4. Ibid.

5. John R. Lee, M.D., *What Your Doctor May Not Tell You About Menopause* (New York: Warner Books, 1996).

CHAPTER 3
THE CHEMICAL EQUATION LINKING BRAIN AND EMOTIONS

1. "Emotional stress leads to immune suppression," *Prevention Magazine* (April 1994): 73–79.

2. Ibid.

3. "Emotional Wrecks," *Health Magazine* (January/February 1999): 70.

4. Information in the section on disorders has been adapted with permission from informational pamphlets from Anxiety Disorders Association of America (ADAA), www.adaa.org.

CHAPTER 4
OVERCOMING THE EFFECT OF STRESS ON YOUR BRAIN

1. Hans Seyle, *Stress Without Distress* (New York: New American Library, 1995).

2. Ordering information: (800) ANXIETY, Monday through Friday, 9 A.M. to 5 P.M.

3. This material has been adapted from "Stress busters from nature," *Natural Health Magazine* (November/December 1998): 168–172.

4. Ibid.

5. Ibid.

6. If you are interested in learning more about 5-HTP, I highly recommend the book *5-HTP: Nature's Serotonin Solution,* by Ray Sahelian, MD (New York: Avery Publishing Group, 1998).

7. Linda Rector Page, "Sugar and Substitutes, Are They

All Bad?" *Healthy Healing–a Guide to Self-Healing for Everyone* (Carmel Valley, CA: 2000), 69.

8. H. J. Roberts, *Aspartame: Is It Safe?* (n.p.: Charles Press, 1990).

9. Linda Rector Page, "Personality Perils of Sugar," *Healthy Healing,* 11th Edition (n. p.: Traditional Wisdom, Inc., 2000), 170.

10. Kari Watson, *The Brain's Balancing Act* (n.p., n. d.).

11. Page, *Healthy Healing.*

12. You may obtain lecithin from Lewis Laboratories International, Ltd., 49 Richmondville Ave., Westport, CT 06880.

13. Joseph Hibbeln, M.D., "When it's good to have a fat head," National Institute on Alcohol Abuse and Alcoholism.

14. Lisa James, "Other brain helpers," *Energy Times* (September 2000): 61–63. Adapted from Lisa James, *Care and Feeding of the Adult Brain.*

CHAPTER 5
STEPS TO A HEALTHY BRAIN

1. *Lancet* 355 (April 15, 2000): 1315–9.

2. "Medicine in the New Millennium," *Daytona Beach News Journal,* January 22, 2000.

3. Harold Bloomfield, *Healing Anxiety with Herbs* (New York: HarperCollins Publishers, 1998).

4. Ibid.

5. Quote from Candace Pert, Ph.D., taken from Sahley, *GABA: The Anxiety Amino Acid,* 34.

6. The Original Bach Flower Essences®, "Questionnaire &

Guide to Your Own Personal Formula," Nelson Bach USA, Ltd., (800) 319-9151, www.nelsonbach.com.

7. The Bach Flower Essences questionnaire and guide to your own personal formula is reprinted by permission of Nelson Bach, USA, Ltd. All of the mentioned Bach Flower Essences can be purchased at health food stores in the United States or by calling (800) 319-9151. The Web site address is www.NelsonBach.com.

CHAPTER 7
AS A MAN THINKETH

1. *Self* magazine (September 1999): 73.

2. James Allen, *As a Man Thinketh* (Marina deKey, CA: DeVoss and Company, n.d.).

3. Dean Ornish, *Love & Survival: 8 Pathways to Intimacy and Health,* (New York: HarperCollins, 1999).

4. Ibid.

5. Kevin Lane Turner, *Your Heart: A Journey to the Other Side of Life* (Ashley Down Publishing Company, 1995).

6. Adapted from Steven James, *Totally Subjective Non-Scientific Guide to Illness and Health*, listed in Bernie Siegel, M.D., *Peace, Love and Healing* (San Francisco, CA: Harper and Row, 1989).

7. Paavo Airola, Ph.D., N.D., *Every Woman's Book* (Phoenix, AZ: Health Plus Publications, 1992).

8. "Forgive to Live," *Health Magazine* (July/August 2000): 28.

CHAPTER 8
BAN CLUTTERED THINKING

1. Deepak Chopra, M.D., "Can I get my dad back?,"

Natural Health Magazine (September/October 1997): 204.

2. "Anger: Lightning Inside," *Megiddo Message*, vol. 87 (December 2000): 12.

3. Ellen Michaud, "Discover the power of forgiveness," *Prevention* magazine (January 1999): 111–163.

4. Adapted from, "Enright Forgiveness Inventory," short version, *Prevention Magazine* (January 1999): 163.

5. Bernie S. Siegel, M.D., *Peace, Love and Healing: Body/ Mind Communication* and *The Path to Self-Healing: An Exploration,* (New York: Harper & Row, 1989), 164–165.

6. Ibid.

7. T. D. Jakes, *The Lady, Her Lover and Her Lord* (New York: G.P. Putnam's Sons, 1998), 204.

CHAPTER 9
A WORK IN PROGRESS

1. Frances J. Norberts, *Come Away My Beloved* (Ojai, CA: King's Farspan, Inc., 1970), 18.

2. Peter Jaret, *Health Magazine* (March 1998): 48–49.

3. Mary Ellin Lerner, "Dangerous emotion news flash," *USA Weekend* (September 8–10, 2000): 4.

4. Terry Shepherd Freidmann, *Freedom Through Health* (Scottsdale, AZ: Harvest Publishing, 1998), 34–37.

5. "The golden years are truly golden," *American Health* (February 1999): 20.

6. "Giggles are Good," *Health Magazine* (October 2000): 76–82.

CHAPTER 10
REACH OUT TO OTHERS

1. Estroff Marano, "Friends for life," *American Health* (February 1999): 55–56.

2. Edward M. Hallowell, "Friends: self-test," *Prevention Magazine* (December 2000).

3. Jane Meredith Adams, "Oh, anxious me," *Health Magazine* (October 2000): 126–132.

CHAPTER 11
USE THE EMOTIONAL RECOVERY ACTION PLAN

1. The script for the relaxation tape has been adapted from pages 22–25 of the *Anti-Aging Booklet* by Rodale Press.

CHAPTER 12
DIFFUSE YOUR EMOTIONAL TIME BOMB AND REGAIN YOUR HEALTH

1. Mary Ellen Lerner, "Anxiety," *USA Weekend* (September 29–October 1, 2000).

2. All emotional links to disease have been adapted from Louise L. Hay, *Heal Your Body* (Santa Monica, CA: Hay House, Inc., 1984).

3. For more information about the thyroid self-test, see Broda O. Barnes, M.D., Lawrence Galton, *Hypothyroidism: The Unsuspected Illness* (New York: Cromwell, 1976).

APPENDIX A
TESTIMONIALS

Being a type A person, I was suffering from frequent nightly anxiety attacks, several of which landed me in the local emergency room at the hospital with symptoms of chest pain, shortness of breath and headaches. The hospital doctors gave me all kinds of tests for my symptoms, which all proved negative, but the symptoms were very real. The end result was no answers, and this increased my anxiety even more.

I called Dr. Maccaro and explained my symptoms and recent experiences. She understood my dilemma and told me that men sometimes have this anxiety problem in the middle of the night. She recommended that I send for information from the Pain and Stress Center in San Antonio, Texas. Dr. Maccaro also recommended that I start taking the supplement GABA on an as-needed basis.

I started taking GABA along with reading the information from the Stress Center, and immediately my nightly attacks stopped. Now, I only use the GABA when my stress level increases, and this does the job completely! Thanks, Dr. Maccaro.

—ROBERT FRANK
DAYTONA BEACH, FL

I'd like to say that when I met Dr. Janet, it was on a wonderful beach trip in Aruba and I was feeling fine. But by the time I found Dr. Janet, I was a basket case. I had lost a ton of weight and looked like death warmed over. I was not sure if I was really alive. My family of two wonderful kids and my adoring wife carried our family unit for months at a time. My parents would come by my store and find me out back in a lounge chair sleeping and soaking up sunshine and shivering. They weren't really sure if I was alive.

I was up and walking when I had to be, but that was only by pure will power and/or stupidity. I opened my store and stayed at least until my manager showed up a half-hour later. I actually prayed that no customers would come in for me to wait on. At 9:00 A.M., I would either leave and go home, or worse, I would stay in the back of my store where I have a patio deck set up. With a lounge chair pointed toward the sun, I'd lie down with my upper body propped up so I could just vegetate and soak up massive quantities of pure Florida sunshine. I'd do that for about three hours until I could get up enough strength to go home and go to bed. I was a useless human being. I was an unproductive member of society. I hate to admit this, but I did think about cashing in a very large life insurance policy for my family, but I couldn't think of a way to take myself out of the game.

My name is Ira; I am forty-seven years old, and I have a small business with two employees. Twelve months ago I came down with something that was crippling me and my lifestyle. I had no energy and could hardly get out of bed in the morning. The thick, smelly sweat through my pores told me this was more than just perspiration. I was freezing and shivering. I was able to crawl out of bed and into the shower. I sat on the floor of the shower because I didn't have enough strength to stand. I didn't eat because I didn't have an appetite. There were other physical symptoms that helped cause my body to shut down. The biggest problems were the depression and fear, which were causing my anxiety over everything that affected my life. I would worry about everything from paying my bills to the kids being able to get to school. I would even break down and cry uncontrollably.

Eventually I went to the emergency room because I had gotten to the point where I was dehydrated. The doctors diagnosed me with a prostate infection. They filled me with fluids and Demerol and antibiotics. I went to my family physician, who diagnosed me with a urinary tract infection. I was on a heavy concentration of multiple kinds of antibiotics for almost three months. I even tried acupuncture treatments. Well, it would have almost been all right, except I was not feeling any better. I still had most of my symptoms and all of my anxiety. My physician prescribed a drug called Paxil to help reduce my stress level, but between the Paxil and the antibiotics, I had an adverse reaction that caused another trip to the emergency room.

On a visit to my local health food store for some vitamins and some hope, I heard of this woman, Dr. Janet Maccaro, who lived in town and had written a remarkably helpful book. I called her and met with her. She suggested a strict comprehensive diet including vitamins, minerals, enzymes, amino acids and adrenals. She also gave me homework. She made me remember and write down what led to my illness. My memory brought me to the first week of December and a big fight with my twenty-two-year-old daughter just after Thanksgiving that caused me tons of stress and anxiety. I also remembered being in the care of medical doctors for five months before meeting Dr. Maccaro.

By Memorial Day, I started to implement her plan for wellness. Within one week I started feeling better. By the Fourth of July, I thought I was cured, but Dr. Janet had other plans for me. She put me on Phase II of her wellness plan. I could now start cutting back on some of my supplements and consolidate some things. I'd like to think that I owe it all to one thing, like GABA or maybe Core Level Adrenal tablets or maybe just the fact that she took me off sugar and put me on Stevia. Either way Dr. Janet gave me a health-building plan that got me healthy and feeling alive and productive. She did for me what a team of other doctors could not.

It's been a whole twelve months now, and I can truthfully say I feel pretty good. I have a bad day sometimes, but that is usually because I got a little lax on my plan or ate too much candy. Sometimes I forget to take my supplements, especially on Sunday, but I always remember to take my GABA.

Dr. Janet asked me to put some words together for her new book. I knew she was writing about GABA and I love it, but I can't honestly say that it was the only thing that did the trick for me.

Right now I am taking only four supplements, and one of them is GABA.

What I learned from this whole experience is that I am not terminally unique. Other people just like me have had these symptoms. Some get better, but for the most part they just keep getting misdiagnosed and continue to slide downhill. I am definitely on of the lucky ones. I got my life back. Thanks, Dr. Janet.

—Ira Freedman
Ormond Beach, FL

———————————————■———————————————

My life was filled with emotional and verbal abuse starting in childhood and continuing throughout my twenty-year-long marriage. This abuse devastated my spirit and had begun to destroy my physical body as well. I thought of myself as a gentle, passive person. As such, I found it difficult to create boundaries around myself and to defend myself from these verbal attacks.

The resulting stress left my immune system nonfunctional. My adrenal glands had no reserves. I suffered from fibromyalgia, type 2 diabetes, candida, asthma and bouts of depression and anxiety.

By the time my marriage ended, my body was in a state of disease. A gift of God's grace brought me to Ormond Beach, where I found myself surrounded by loving, kind and knowledgeable friends. Dr. Janet was among them.

Her message about a chemical-free way to lift my anxiety and stop my insomnia was exactly what I needed. I was already doing many things right—practicing forgiveness and becoming increasingly committed to my spiritual life. But there was still a missing piece.

My brain had become unable to produce enough serotonin. Therefore, my total healing was not possible. Dr. Janet explained the function of amino acids and the neurotransmitters in the brain and suggested that a natural amino acid, GABA, could help.

This was the missing piece I needed to complete the puzzle.

When I took her advice, my healing took another great leap. My anxieties subsided, and I was finally able to sleep through the night. My overall feeling of well-being increased to the point at which I was able to discontinue the GABA after four months.

I know that healing is a lifetime challenge and must be met with an open mind and an open heart. Now, I feel as though I have reached a place of balance and clarity. I am grateful to God for many blessings. One of them was meeting Dr. Janet and learning about GABA.

—Name omitted to protect individual's privacy

APPENDIX B
FREE FACT SHEETS

Mail your complete mailing address to:

NIMH Public Inquiries
6001 Executive Blvd. Room 8184
MSC 9663
Bethesda, MD 20892-9662

For fact sheet on: .... Publication No.
Social Phobia OM99-4171
PTSD (Posttraumatic Stress Disorder) OM99-4157
Panic Disorder...........................OM99-4155
OCD (Obsessive Compulsive Disorder)......OM99-4154
GAD (Generalized Anxiety Disorder)........OM99-4153
Anxiety Disorders (General)...............OM99-4152

WHO CAN HELP

Resources:

- The Midwest Center for Stress and Anxiety: (800) ANXIETY. Lucinda Bassett, executive director, tape series Attacking Anxiety and Depression (16 audiocassette tapes and workbook)
- Anxiety Disorders of America (ADAA): (240) 485-1001; 8730 Georgia Ave., Suite 600, Silver Spring, MD 20910; www.adaa.org
- The Pain and Stress Center: (800) 669-2256; 5282 Medical Drive, Ste. 160, San Antonio, TX 78229. Billie J. Sahley, PhD, director
- Nutri-West: (800) 451-5620. Please mention Dr. Janet Maccaro.

APPENDIX C
PRODUCT SOURCES

PROGESTERONE CREAM

I am very excited to share with you two wonderful ways to enhance your new higher level of health. After struggling for twenty years with severe hormonal imbalance and discovering that the reason was an imbalance in my estrogen/progesterone ratio, I am pleased to share with you my formula birthed out of my own quest for hormonal balance and well-being. I call it *Dr. Janet's Balanced by Nature Progesterone Cream*. It contains pure pharmaceutical-grade natural progesterone derived from the Mexican wild yam. In addition, it meets the specifications that John Lee, MD, recommends for an effective cream. I have included the product information and description for you.

If you are experiencing cramps, migraines, bloating, breast tenderness, hot flashes…if you can't lose weight, lack energy, are depressed…if you have mood swings, fibroid tumors, endometriosis, infertility, a family history of female-related cancer, foggy thinking, perimenopause…or if you are losing height, you may be experiencing hormonal imbalance! Dr. Janet's Balanced by Nature Progesterone Cream can help cramps, bloating, depression, mood swings, water retention, hot flashes and decreased libido. It can also prevent osteoporosis and protect against breast fibroids.

Everyone is different. As such, the use of natural progesterone body cream should be adjusted to meet your own needs. The following suggestions are to be used as a guide only. Although there have been no reports of any significant side effects or health problems associated with natural progesterone, consider consulting your physician. Some women notice results right away, while others may see changes in one to three months.

Use the progesterone cream between ovulation until the onset of menses (the time of ovulation can be determined by a dramatic change—rise or fall—in basal body temperature and by changes—thinning or thickening—in vaginal secretions). Some women also experience lower abdominal pains during ovulation. If you have symptoms prior to ovulation (i.e. migraines), you may want to begin using the cream earlier until your period. You don't need natural progesterone during menstruation. However, if you experience cramps or other symptoms during menstruation, you may use the cream until the symptoms are alleviated.

FOR PMS AND MENOPAUSAL SYMPTOMS

After ovulation (days 14–18 after onset of last period), use small amount of cream, no more than ¼ teaspoon once a day. Days 18–23, use ¼ teaspoon twice daily, gradually increasing to ½ teaspoon twice daily. Day 23 until period, use ½ teaspoon twice daily.

FOR OSTEOPOROSIS

Bone density testing is recommended before using natural progesterone. This is to establish a base line from which to measure changes in your bone density every six to twelve months. Consult your healthcare provider. Use ¼–½ teaspoon (for severe cases) daily.

FOR POSTMENOPAUSAL SYMPTOMS

Use cream for three weeks, ¼ to ½ teaspoon twice per day, one week without cream.

Please note: While low-dose natural progesterone creams are generally effective for mild PMS symptoms, it has been found that higher doses (980–1,000 milligrams) of natural progesterone cream have been more effective in balancing a woman's system during premenopause, menopause and postmenopause. This is especially true for the prevention and treatment of osteoporosis.

ARTHRITIS SKIN CREAM

Arthritis can be a real pain! I recommend my arthritis skin cream—Dr. Janet's Balanced by Nature Glucosamine Cream, which contains cutting-edge ingredients used as an ancient natural remedy for arthritis sufferers. It is now widely acknowledged for its effectiveness for the relief of arthritis pain and inflammation.

Bromelain, an enzyme derived from pineapple juice, blocks inflammation by stimulating the production of plasmin, a body compound that aids in the reduction of localized swelling.

No capsicum is used. No extract of hot pepper or cayenne means no burning sensation to the skin! Dr. Janet's Balanced by Nature Glucosamine Cream provides relief from arthritis pain without discomfort.

This high-quality formulation of emu oil, pregnenolone and glucosamine sulfate, along with proper amounts of specially selected herbs, vitamins and enzymes, is the product of years of study and research. It was developed for natural, effective solutions for my clients' continued good health. This has been the goal as well as the result. Blended with a specially formulated cream base, Balanced by Nature Glucosamine Cream is the solution I recommend to my clients for relief of arthritis symptoms, because it works naturally to ease their pain and inflammation from arthritis.

Apply Glucosamine Cream by placing a small amount, approximately ¼ to ½ teaspoon of cream, on your fingertips. Rub gently into the area of your pain, directly onto the skin. If your arthritis pain is located in your joints or covered by a large amount of tissue (i.e. hips, thighs or shoulders), simply increase the amount of cream and apply more generously directly to the joint area. The cream should penetrate, and relief will begin within a minute.

I pass a jar of this unique formulation around to my audience during seminars, and I instruct anyone who is in pain from arthritis, muscle pain, injury and even fibromyalgia to apply this cream. At the fifteen-minute break, I ask how many people are still hurting. Remarkably, almost everyone has gotten relief.

Glucosamine cream is a specially blended combination of

all-natural ingredients. Emu oil, as scientific studies have shown, has been used for thousands of years by Australian aborigines who found this versatile bird to be a valuable resource for natural, effective relief from pain. Muscle pain and sunburn pain, as well as inflammation in joints, can be relieved as a result of two substances that occur naturally in the oil itself, lenolenic acid (the painkiller) and oleic acid (an anti-inflammatory). The natural properties of the oil of emu are so simple and nonintrusive that our skin has no need for resistance to it. Therefore the oil is permitted to simply pass through the skin layer without interruption, providing the immediate benefit of pain relief for you!

Balanced by Nature products are made with the highest grade of quality ingredients; only the most expensive oils, virtually odorless and colorless, are used.

Pregnenolone is a natural hormone produced by the body when cholesterol is broken down in the mitochondria of the cell. This remarkable process occurs naturally in the brain and adrenal glands. Scientific and medical studies have shown that as we age, our levels of pregnenolone decline although the balance of natural hormones, such as pregnenolone, is essential to our optimum good health. While pregnenolone is not found naturally in plants, it can be manufactured naturally from plants. The wild yam, native to Mexico and China, is the common and reliable source for natural pregnenolone production.

Used successfully for more than fifty years for the effective relief of the pain and inflammation of arthritis, pregnenolone also helps reduce the swelling and stiffness associated with arthritis pain. Studies have shown that the use of natural pregnenolone supplement also contributes to significant improvement in memory, task performance and a general sense of well-being.

Glucosamine sulfate is a substance found naturally in your body. It is a combination of sugar and amine. As a natural constituent of cartilage that stimulates the production of connective tissue in your body, glucosamine production slows in the body as we age. This leaves the cartilage unable to retain water and thereby reduces the shock-absorber effect we enjoyed with healthier cartilage when proper levels were naturally produced by the body. Glucosamine sulfate works to lubricate your joints, rebuild damaged cartilage and stimulate the production of new cartilage.

Boswellin is a natural extract from the herb boswellia, used as an ancient natural remedy for arthritis sufferers. It is now widely acknowledged for its cutting-edge benefits and effectiveness for the relief of arthritis pain and inflammation.

PRODUCT SOURCE LIST

Most products listed below can be found in most health food stores. For those that are not available in health food stores, I have provided contact information.

Dr. Janet's Balanced by Nature

For information or to order, call (800) 231-8485 or go to www.drjanetphd.com.

- Dr. Janet's Balanced by Nature Progesterone Cream
- Dr. Janet's Balanced by Nature Glucosamine Cream

Health food stores

- GABA
- Carlson's Magnesium Gel Caps
- Kyo-Green by Wakunaga
- CalMax Powder
- Rescue Remedy

Nutri-West

Call (800) 451-5620 to order. You will need to mention Dr. Janet Maccaro.

- Core Level Adrenal Glandular

THE PAIN AND STRESS CENTER

Call (800) 669-2256 to order.

- Liquid Serotonin
- Brain Link
- Anxiety Control 24

THE MIDWEST CENTER FOR STRESS AND ANXIETY

Call (800) ANXIETY for information and to order.

- Attacking Anxiety and Depression tape series

BIBLIOGRAPHY

Books

Allen, James. *As a Man Thinketh*. Mariner de Key, CA: DeVoss and Company.

Bloomfield, Harold. *Healing Anxiety with Herbs* (New York: HarperCollins, 1998).

Crook, W. G., MD. *Yeast Screening, the Yeast Connection,* first edition. Jackson, TN: Professional Books, 1983.

Friedmann, Terry Shepherd, MD. *Emotions Translate into the Physical.* N.p.: *Freedom through Health,* n.d.

Fuller, DicQie. *The Healing Power of Enzymes.* N.p.: Forbes Custom Publishing, 1998.

Hay, Louise, L. *Heal Your Body.* Santa Monica, CA: Hay House, Inc., 1984.

Hibblen, Joseph, MD. "When it's good to have a fat head." National Institute on Alcohol Abuse and Alcoholism.

Jakes, Bishop T. D. *The Lady, Her Lover and Her Lord.* New York: G. P. Putnam's Sons, 1998.

Lee, John R., MD. *What Your Doctor May Not Tell You About Menopause.* New York: Warner Books, 1996.

Norberts, Frances J. *Release Thy Grief, Come Away My Beloved.* Ojar, CA: King's Farspan, Inc.

Ornish, Dean. *Love and Survival: Eight Pathways to Intimacy and Health.* New York: HarperCollins, 1998.

225

Page, Linda. "Personality Perils of Sugar." *Healthy Healing,* 11th Edition. March 2000. Traditional Wisdom, Inc.

Paavo, Airola, PhD. *Every Woman's Book.* Phoenix, AZ: Health Plus Publishers, 1992.

Sahley, Billie, PhD. *Anxiety Epidemic.* San Antonio, TX: Pain and Stress Center, 1994.

——. *Chronic Emotional Fatigue.* San Antonio, TX: Pain and Stress Center, 2000.

——. *GABA:The Anxiety Amino Acid.* San Antonio, TX: Pain and Stress Center, 1998.

Sahelian, Ray, MD. *Nature's Serotonin Solution* (New York: Avery Publishing Group, 1998). This book provides more information about 5-HTP.

Siegal, Bernie S., MD. *Peace, Love, and Healing.* New York: Harper and Row, 1989.

Turner, Kevin Lane. *The Pursuit of Happiness: A Journey to the Other Side of Life.* Dallas, TX: Ashley Down Publishing Company, 1995.

——. *Your Heart: A Journey to the Other Side of Life.* Dallas, TX: Ashley Down Publishing Company, 1995.

Magazine articles

Chopra, Deepak, MD. "Can I get my dad back?" *Natural Health Magazine,* September/October 1997.

Galland, Leo, MD. "When Stress Shatters, Magnesium Saves." *Great Life,* October 1998.

Hallowell, Edward M., MD. "Friends; self-test." *Prevention Magazine* December 2000.

James, Lisa. "Other brain helpers." *Energy Times,* September 2000. Adapted from Lisa James. *Care and Feeding of the Adult Brain.*

Lerner, Mary Ellin. "Anxiety." *USA Weekend.* September 29-October 1, 2000.

Marano, Hara Estroff. "Children of Divorce Twenty-five Years Later." *USA Weekend,* September 15–19, 2000.

Ornish, Dean. "The second act of Dean Ornish" *Natural Health Magazine,* November/December 1998.

Watson, Kari. "A strain on the brain is felt mostly as a drain." *Natural Health Magazine,* September/October 1998.

n.a. "Dangerous emotion news flash." *USA Weekend,* September 8–10, 2000.

n.a. "Emotional stress leads to immune suppression." *Prevention Magazine,* April 1994.

n.a. "Emotional wrecks." *Health Magazine,* January/February 1999.

n.a. "Forgive to live." *Health Magazine,* July/August 2000.

n.a. "Giggles are Good." *Health Magazine,* October 2000.

n.a. "The golden years are truly golden." *American Health,* February 1999, page 20.

n.a. "The healing balm of acceptance." *American Health,* February 1999.

n.a. "Mind/body news flash," *Self,* September 1999.

n.a. "7 Dangerous Habits of Highly Anxious People." *Health Magazine,* October 2000.

n.a. "Stress busters from nature." *Natural Health Magazine,* November/December 1998.

n.a. "Working on your night moves: sleep deep without drugs." *More,* September/October 1999.

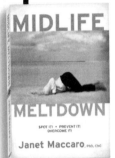

Strang Communications, the publisher of both Charisma House and *Charisma* magazine, wants to give you 3 FREE ISSUES of our award-winning magazine.

Since its inception in 1975, *Charisma* magazine has helped thousands of Christians stay connected with what God is doing worldwide.

Within its pages you will discover in-depth reports and the latest news from a Christian perspective, biblical health tips, global events in the body of Christ, personality profiles, and so much more. Join the family of *Charisma* readers who enjoy feeding their spirit each month with miracle-filled testimonies and inspiring articles that bring clarity, provoke prayer, and demand answers.

To claim your **3 free issues** of *Charisma,* send your name and address to: Charisma 3 Free Issue Offer, 600 Rinehart Road, Lake Mary, FL 32746. Or you may call 1-800-829-3346 and ask for Offer # 93FREE. This offer is only valid in the USA.

---

www.charismamag.com